What Your Colleagues Are S̶____ ____

"In the midst of this racialized, difficult moment in the history of American schools, this book provides leaders with language, tools, and a framework to unleash positive social change. Understanding and applying the concepts Dr. Milner offers will strengthen leadership for racial and social justice, thus improving outcomes for all children."

Shawn Joseph, Former Superintendent
in Delaware and Tennessee
Co-Director, AASA/Howard University
Urban Superintendent's Academy

"Every school leader needs to read this truth-telling book. In a time where so many are steering away from issues of race, racism, and the harms inflicted on the lives of Black and Brown students in schools, Dr. Milner instead confronts these important topics while helping leaders to develop race-conscious thinking and anti-racist practices. He beautifully and organically blends theory, research, history, and practical approaches for cultivating leaders' minds toward advancing justice for the hope of our humanity. The content in this book is so moving and MUST be the new model for how we prepare the next generation of leaders."

Gholdy Muhammad, Associate Professor,
University of Illinois, Chicago

"Dr. Milner expertly provides a comprehensive examination into how racism operates within schools and society before delivering evidence-based leadership approaches and strategies that advance racial justice. In this timely and engaging text written for practitioners and aspiring leaders, Dr. Milner takes racism head on by clearly outlining how school leaders in solidarity with educators and communities can recognize, confront, and root out racial injustice. Frontline Leadership provides a unique and powerful framework for strategic and concerted action that is not only about disrupting the status quo and challenging white supremacy, but also advancing schooling practices that are racially just and contribute to the well-being and success of the entire school community. For educators and leaders who feel silenced or paralyzed amid culture wars and right-wing attacks on public education, *The Race Card* is a must-read because it provides valuable practitioner-oriented strategies that cultivate and sustain racial justice in schools and communities."

David DeMatthews, Associate Professor,
University of Texas at Austin

"Dr. Milner gifts the world with *The Race Card* during a time of racial and social crisis. *The Race Card* boldly centers and conceptualizes the indispensable role of race in educational leadership, while U.S. society opts for colorblindness, anti-Black sentiment, and white supremacy in educational and social structures. Dr. Milner systematically rebukes and rejects these notions, and demonstrates how these ever-present destructive social structures crush the potential for educational systems to serve students of color. Instead, Milner proposes an informative and instructive framework for an equitable leadership paradigm in which all students can succeed. A must-read for educational leaders, *The Race Card* provides definitions and research that informs school leaders of how to engage in Frontline Leadership in order to establish just and equitable leadership practices in U.S. schools."

Lisa Bass Freeman, Associate Professor,
North Carolina State University

The Race Card

This book is dedicated to the loving memory of my sheroes:

Annie Domineck

Gail McCutcheon

Eunice Milner

Annie Mae Stanley

Annie Lou Sutton

Annie Maude Williams

Corine Williams

I am because of you!

The Race Card

Leading the Fight for
Truth in America's Schools

H. Richard Milner IV

Foreword by Mark Anthony Gooden

FOR INFORMATION:

Corwin

A SAGE Company

2455 Teller Road

Thousand Oaks, California 91320

(800) 233-9936

www.corwin.com

SAGE Publications Ltd.

1 Oliver's Yard

55 City Road

London EC1Y 1SP

United Kingdom

SAGE Publications India Pvt. Ltd.

Unit No 323-333, Third Floor, F-Block

International Trade Tower Nehru Place

New Delhi 110 019

SAGE Publications Asia-Pacific Pte. Ltd.

18 Cross Street #10-10/11/12

China Square Central

Singapore 048423

President: Mike Soules

Vice President and
  Editorial Director: Monica Eckman

Program Director
  and Publisher: Dan Alpert

Senior Content Development
  Editor: Lucas Schleicher

Content Development
  Editor: Mia Rodriguez

Editorial Assistant: Natalie Delpino

Production Editor: Tori Mirsadjadi

Copy Editor: Colleen Brennan

Typesetter: C&M Digitals (P) Ltd.

Proofreaders: Dennis Webb and Theresa Kay

Indexer: Integra

Cover Designer: Scott Van Atta

Marketing Manager: Melissa Duclos

Printed in Canada

Paperback ISBN 978-1-0719-0777-1

This book is printed on acid-free paper

23 24 25 26 27 10 9 8 7 6 5 4 3 2 1

Contents

Chapter 3. How to Co-Develop Systematic Plans and Designs   67

Chapter 4. How to Disrupt Punishment and Pushout Practices 95

Chapter 5. No Turning Back: Conclusions, Summaries, Recommendations, and Implications 125

Foreword

What Does Racism Have to Do With Frontline Leadership?

By Mark Anthony Gooden

About 10 years ago, I was inspired to write an article that asked what racism had to do with leadership. The title was inspired by two occurrences. The first was a conversation with an African American colleague who was a leader in higher education with a background in business. After attending a leadership seminar together, she shared her belief that good leadership was just good leadership and race had nothing to do with it. Needless to say, I was confused and inspired by that response. Second, the title was inspired by Tina Turner's anti-love hit song, "What's Love Got to Do With It?" Like the title of this song, my article was an anti-racism expression because I essentially argued through a critical race theory (CRT) analysis that racism is absolutely in leadership and that we should fight vigorously (as anti-racists) to counter the idea of color-blind or color-evasive leadership. To carefully construct this argument, I applied CRT specifically to the work of two Black principals and their race-informed and troubling portrayals in two different movies (Gooden, 2012). My central point then was that it was nearly impossible to properly examine and improve the urban principalship (or any for that matter) without some conceptualization of race and racism in the U.S. context.

In *this book*, Milner uses powerful personal narratives and experiences and compelling research to remind us that race and racism are obviously still here today and impacting leadership. Leaders cannot lead effectively in the fight against inequity without grasping an understanding that race is always within them and the society that they work in every day. It's worth noting that his definition of leaders goes beyond position and includes young people who he wants to prepare in this fight for racial justice. From the start, Milner reminds us that attempting to lead without this acknowledgment is not only wrong, but it is dangerous and particularly harmful to the development of students, teachers, staff, and other leaders in the building. Also, this injury extends to many communities that have been impacted by racism, whether they shout out this fact or not. As Milner notes, it can be devastating for young people and adults alike as whites freely practice normalized behaviors that cause profound harm against racialized bodies.

To that end, Milner leads the reader through a focused and fruitful discussion, first seeking to teach what racism has to do with leadership in 2023. To do so, he introduces two more concepts from the literature that should be helpful in deepening the understanding of readers. Accordingly, Milner adds the interconnected concepts of whiteness and the notion of anti-Blackness as in his discussion of leadership. Both of these drivers of inequity are imperative yet underexplored concepts in the study of race and leadership. That's a shame because so much of leaders' training is based on rational, technical, and color-evasive approaches that normalize white ways of engaging in organizations. The disturbing normalizing of white supremacy is also pulled into this discussion, which lays bare all its harms.

Moreover, the study of anti-Blackness is important to help folks understand deeply ingrained disdain for Black people. Anti-Blackness pushes above and beyond general forms of racism. Anti-Blackness violently harms Black people. These troubling approaches to leadership and their alignment with compliance often seek out Black bodies, frequently and systematically aiming to label them as perpetrators, misfits, outsiders, or criminals. Anti-Black racism then needs to be explored to help us contextually understand our question about what racism has to do with leadership. In short, we are reminded that school punishment practices are often anti-Black. Who is responsible for implementing those anti-Black systems? You guessed it, leaders; and in many cases, Black men who have been charged with the duty of chief compliance officers. Indeed, many of them have found it difficult to advance beyond the position of assistant principal or overseers of Black children's compliance.

To address this issue and so many others, Milner employs the concept of Frontline Leadership as an analytical tool. This approach grows out of highlights of structural hierarchy of first responders responsible for the health, vitality, and success of the organization. There is an emphasis on implementing a focused system of goals and feedback, reminding the reader that not only is deconstructing systems necessary but reconstructing them is needed as well, and this process cannot happen without the commitment of capable leaders.

To build on the concept of Frontline Leadership, Milner presents eight tenets to assist the reader in grasping and organizing these big ideas. While I decline to enumerate them here, it's worth summarizing some of them as they outline his approaches to Frontline Leadership. These include calls to be familiar with research, disrupt race-blindness, support hard work but challenge the meritocracy myth, revise punishment systems, learn, and develop daily, among others. He also challenges directly some myths that leaders will need to reflect upon. Leaders will do well to broaden their thinking about these possibilities as they thoughtfully help them study and map the complexities of education. Each myth (or lie) is followed by potential outcomes and opportunity gaps that many leaders will undoubtedly find as useful.

Milner's conceptualization of Frontline Leadership leans toward centering racial justice in leadership practice, which is an idea I have agreed with for all my career and advocated for, especially in principal leadership (Gooden & Dantley, 2012). While this fact is apparent throughout this book, it is captured very well in his requirement that these leaders pose these questions in the learning environment. These questions nudge Frontline leaders to examine what privileges they are willing to sacrifice in the co-creation of a racially just context that serves people of color. It also asks to what degree do they advance racial justice when I perceive benefits for my own person and collective (white community) affordances.

As one can imagine, such questions make it impossible for a leader to deny that racism has something to do with leadership. More importantly, the questions mentioned in this foreword—like *this book*—give readers a positive way forward in Frontline Leadership and provide access to a set of well-honed tools to help educators understand this connection while learning how to fight for racial justice. I hope you find the rich content here as exciting as I did and that you embrace it as we prepare young people to advocate for a more racially just future.

References

Gooden, M. A. (2012). What does racism have to do with leadership? Countering the idea of color-blind leadership: A reflection on race and the growing pressures of the urban principalship. *Journal of Educational Foundations, 26*(1–2), 67–84.

Gooden, M. A., & Dantley, M. (2012). Centering race in a framework for leadership preparation. *Journal of Research on Leadership in Education, 7*(2), 235–251.

Acknowledgments

I am so thankful to my wife, Shelley, who is my best friend, my Light, my rock, my every single thing. Shelley designs our life together in a way that brings me more joy than I ever thought imaginable. Thank you for believing in this book and me. And thank you for being the best mother to our daughters.

I also thank my daughters, Anna and Elise, for being so patient with me as I balanced much to finish this book project. Anna: thank you for your confidence, courage, and growth over the years. You are so bright, caring, and capable. Elise: thank you for taking up the writing "gene" from me. I cannot wait to read your bestseller someday. You are so bright, athletic, and empathetic. I am honored to be Anna and Elise's dad.

Along with my siblings, Tanya and Reginald, I carry with me the legacy and excellence of my parents, Henry III and Barbara. And special acknowledgment of my mother-in-law, Margaret Banks.

What I know for sure is that, through all my efforts and achievements, I am most proud of being Shelley's husband, Anna and Elise's daddy, Henry and Barbara's son, and Tanya and Reginald's brother.

Finally, there is no way I could have pulled this book project together had it not been for the support and encouragement of Dan Alpert and Lucas Schleicher from Corwin. And to every single young person, educator, community member, colleague, policymaker, advocate, family member, and friend who has taught and encouraged me: thank you! I acknowledge and appreciate you all.

About the Author

H. Richard Milner IV (also known as Rich) is Cornelius Vanderbilt Chair of Education and Joseph A. Johnson, Jr. Distinguished Leadership Professor in the Department of Teaching and Learning at Vanderbilt University. He has courtesy appointments in the Department of Leadership, Policy, and Organizations and the Department of Sociology. Professor Milner is the founding Director of the Initiative for Race Research and Justice at Vanderbilt. A researcher, scholar, and teacher, Dr. Milner is President of the American Educational Research Association (AERA), the largest educational research organization in the world. He is an elected member of the National Academy of Education and a Fellow of AERA. Dr. Milner has published more than 100 scholarly journal articles and book chapters, and he has published seven books, two of which are bestsellers. His work has been cited or featured in the *New York Times,* the *Los Angeles Times*, and the *Atlantic*. Dr. Milner has taught high school language arts and developmental reading in community college and has been a substitute teacher. He has served on faculty at several universities, including the University of Pittsburgh and York University in Toronto.

Introduction

1

//

A few years ago, a group of parents, community members, and policy advocates invited me to share recommendations from my research about ways to support minoritized communities in education. This diverse, but mostly white, group was concerned about racial unrest and potential backlash after the killing of George Floyd at the hand of the state. "Liberal minded" and "forward thinking" were the words used by the group to describe themselves to me prior to and during my visit with them. They prepped me by sharing that they did not want to focus on race or the Floyd murder, *per se*, but on poverty, economic disparities, drug addiction, and lack of opportunities for many in their community. They preferred and guided me to prepare my presentation for a much broader conversation about "minority groups," and they wanted specific recommendations about ways to help students "do better" in schools. They pleaded: we must do something in our communities and especially our schools to quell the injustices and social unrest facing the nation. Moreover, they were concerned about deep political divisions and lack of solidarity that seemed to be tearing up the United States of America.

Maintaining my professional obligation and commitment to equity, I prepared and focused my remarks on Black students, students living below the poverty line, students whose first language was not English, recent immigrant students, Muslim students, and LGBTQIA+ students. I also attempted to focus on important and necessary intersections of these students' experiences and identities as I invited those in attendance to imagine equitable policies and practices. In fact, I talked with the group about many of the issues I explore within and throughout the pages of this book.

Drawing from well-substantiated research, I attempted to map and share with the group complexities of the issues we face as a nation, sprinkled with recommendations on what they could (and should!) do in solidarity to make society and schools better. But it appeared that the group wanted simple, fixed, and definitive answers. And they wanted solutions disconnected from the *realness of racism*. Racism is not a playing matter. Racism is serious, as it hurts and harms the bodies and capacities of those who experience it—young people, educators, families, and communities.

As I presented, those in attendance engaged in sidebar conversations with and among each other reflecting on the data, insights, and recommendations I shared on slides. Although I could not hear their comments between and among themselves during my presentation, their concern became clear to me. After I finished my presentation the very first comment from a participant (with head nods from most of the others in the room) was, "This presentation feels like you are 'playing the race card.'" A bit stunned and disappointed by the comment, my response was firm and resolute and sets the stage for this book: "Yes, I certainly am." *Play the race card*. School leadership committed to centering racial justice requires that we amplify and intensify focus on race, not shy away from it. I reflected: Why should I somehow lie about, move away from, or be afraid to speak truth in this space (or any space) about the lingering and enduring effects of racism in society and education? Moreover, what does it mean to "play the race card," and who decides when such a card is being played? Why do some people feel uncomfortable or disconnected from discourse, interactions, policies, and practices when issues of race and racism are interrogated in the United States?

> Why should I somehow lie about, move away from, or be afraid to speak truth about the lingering and enduring effects of racism in society and education?

The general sentiment in the room was that when we "play the race card," deeper divisions emerge. Although they had good intentions, the group wanted me to placate and ponder to a group of unnamed Americans whom they believed they needed on their side to make social progress. These Americans were those who did not want to think, talk, or engage in race but, in the eyes of the participants, "good [liberal] people" who could help advance our agenda of educational opportunity for all. They wanted to repair the social unrest in America, which was precipitated by racism, whiteness, and anti-Black racism, by not engaging in these very issues that brought us to this moment. How can we address racism and improve policies and practices in schools and society when we do not "play the race card"?

> They wanted to repair the social unrest in America, which was precipitated by racism, whiteness, and anti-Black racism, by not engaging in these very issues that brought us to this moment.

Also, when one suggests that another is "playing a race card," it sends the message that the race card player is somehow being deceptive, disingenuous, conniving, and unfair. I disagree with this view of what it means to play the race card. When people invoke race and racism in the spirit of improving conditions for young people and other minoritized communities, there is nothing deceptive or disingenuous about naming the conditions that continue to hurt and harm. So, yes, we must play the race card.

What I call opportunity imperatives (Figure 1.1) capture many of the issues I covered during my presentation. I invite readers of this book, and school leaders specifically, to consider the breadth and depth of these issues and their intersecting relationships to race and racism. Although this list is not exhaustive, school leaders must understand the complexities of the matters in Figure 1.1 to make schools more welcoming, restorative, transformative, healing, and racially just spaces.

FIGURE 1.1   Opportunity Imperatives

The over-referral of Black and Brown and other minoritized students to the office to punish them for "misbehavior"	The serious effects of poverty on student outcomes	Poor collaborations and partnerships between schools and the families and communities they serve	"Pushout" and the disproportionate suspensions and expulsions
The underrepresentation and under-enrollment of Black and Brown students in STEM areas	The low (and declining) numbers of teachers of color in the teaching force	The cradle-to-school-to-prison intersection	Myths about the achievement and socialization of Asian American students as "models"
Institutionally induced mental, psychological, emotional strain of minoritized bodies	Underprepared (yet committed) educators for the "new" political landscape	Threats/discourse to end affirmative action	The narrowing of curriculum that pushes out the arts in classrooms and in schools
Increases in gun violence and the need for school safety	Opportunity gaps across disciplines masked in the language of achievement gaps	Book banning and curriculum censorship	Marginalization of LGBTQIA+ students
	Poor and inadequate funding		

To be sure, all the issues in Figure 1.1 intersect with issues of race and racism—a central focus of this book. And school leaders should "play the race card" in their quest to study, design, and improve tools, mechanisms, systems, policies, and practices to help our students have a chance at experiencing more humanizing educational contexts.

As I presented to the group, I explicitly (and unapologetically) focused on race, racism, whiteness, and anti-Black racism. Put simply, I played the race card—at least in the minds and hearts of those in attendance. And I firmly support leadership practices that play the race card.

But What Do I Mean by Race?

Critical race theorists have argued that race and racism are everywhere, operating at all times, and that—perhaps most importantly—racism is a permanent dimension of the fabric of U.S. society (Ladson-Billings & Tate, 1995) and education (Milner, 2020a, 2020b). It is well-accepted and understood that race is socially constructed (Bennett et al., 2019; Boutte, 2016; Farinde-Wu, 2018; Gooden & O'Doherty, 2014; Laughter, 2018; Milner, 2015; Sealey-Ruiz, 2016). In addition, race is phenotypically and physically constructed (Fergus, 2017; Harper & Donnor, 2017; McGee et al., 2016; Monroe, 2013; Singer, 2016). That is, in constructing race, people examine and interpret the physicality and outside, phenotypical markers of individuals. Race is also contextually, geographically, place-centered, and spatially constructed (Alvarez, 2017; Green, 2015; Morris & Monroe, 2009; Pearman, 2020; Tate, 2008; Williams, 2018). For instance, race is conceptualized differently across continents and space. Race is also legally constructed (Bell, 2004; Harris, 1993; Lynn & Dixson, 2022), as laws and policies influence what we know and do in society. And race is historically constructed (Alridge, 2003; Anderson, 1988; Milner & Lomotey, 2014; Walker, 1996), as historical moments and movements such as slavery, eugenics, reconstruction, Jim Crow, redlining, desegregation, and busing influence policy and practice. Still, Leonardo and Manning (2017) explained, "While race is socially constructed, and not 'real' as a scientific classification system, it has real material and affective impact on people: the way they think, speak, and act in the world" (p. 20).

Race is far more than skin color.

It is important to note that *race is far more than skin color*.

Thus, throughout this book, when I refer to race, I am referring to a construct—much more nuanced, deep, robust, and intricate than simply skin color alone. School leaders working to transform their school environments toward racial justice understand they must have and/or possess insights about the constructs, ideas, and ideals they pursue. Race is one of those terms that is often invoked but rarely understood in educational discourse, policy, and practice. This is a problem and must be addressed.

And What Is Racism?

Berman and Paradies (2010) define racism as "that which maintains or exacerbates inequality of opportunity among . . . groups. Racism can be expressed through stereotypes (racist beliefs), prejudice (racist emotions/affect) or discrimination (racist behaviors and practices)" (p. 217). Moreover, racism is a practice of injustice and discrimination that works to maintain white supremacy and the white status quo. It is important to note that racist acts through power may emerge intentionally or unintentionally (Carter, 2007). Whether intentional or unintentional, racism is a vicious practice that can leave people of color in schools, workplaces, and society marginalized and traumatized where white people are assumed to be the ideal norm by which others should be compared or measured. Racism attacks and harms. Racism is an action verb that works through power structures and power moves guided by beliefs and mindsets of people to control the social order.

Having worked with thousands of teachers, young people, family and community members, and school leaders over the years, most of these people have not been intentionally (or even overtly) racist. Educators do not tend to get into the work of teaching to practice racism. However, due to implicit biases, stereotypes, misnomers, unexamined preconceived notions, and historical prejudices that are reified, unintentional racist practices are devastating for young people and adults alike, as white people practice normalized practices that cause profound harm against racially minoritized bodies. Whether intentional or unintentional, racism is real in the lives of people, and school leaders have a chance to help change and transform a racist trajectory of a place or space.

This book is dedicated to helping school leaders bring out the very best of all educators in pursuit of racial justice and the co-creation of school spaces that make a positive difference for all. Although other school leadership books focus on race and racism, I am also including related constructs of whiteness and anti-Black racism as central features of what must be considered in any contemporary effort and agenda leading toward racial justice and racial equity in schools.

But What Is Whiteness?

Race, racism, and whiteness are practically, empirically, and conceptually connected. Race, racism, and whiteness have been conceptualized in relation to place—the ecological nature of schools and communities (Cabrera et al., 2016; Diamond et al., 2021; Milner, 2015, 2020a).

Moreover, studies have examined issues of race, racism, and whiteness in the context of teacher education (Alvarez, 2017; Alvarez & Milner, 2018; Annamma, 2014; Bennett et al., 2019; Milner, 2008; Milner & Howard, 2013; Sleeter, 2017) and mathematics education (Beatty & Leyva, 2016). Beatty and Leyva (2016) advanced three interrelated features—institutional, labor, and identity—in their developing framework to address whiteness in the context of mathematics education. Moving beyond simplistic, myopic framing of whiteness, these researchers argued "whiteness must . . . counteract the mechanisms and institutional ways in which [w]hite supremacy in mathematics education reproduces subordination and advantage" (Beatty & Leyva, 2016, p. 76).

Evans-Winters and Hines (2020) explained that "whiteness is a socially constructed concept that centers white people and white things—whiteness is a person, place, thing and idea. Whiteness is an action word and it is status quo, the norm of society, and cannot exist if there is not [an] element of power, domination, and oppression" (p. 4). Indeed, whiteness is a noun and an action verb. Whiteness is about how white people use their bodies to enact particular kinds of actions and practices. But whiteness can manifest not only through the practices of white people but also through the actions of others as well. In this way, whiteness can be executed and practiced through the bodies of anybody, including people of color. This is why we see so many Black school leaders practicing harmful practices in schools. Castagno (2013) maintained that "whiteness refers to the structural arrangements and ideologies of racial dominance within the United States. Racial power and inequities are at the core of whiteness, but all forms of power and inequity create and perpetuate whiteness" (p. 101). As communities of color embrace ideological, historical, contemporary, and otherwise paradigmatic ways of knowing and being, they too can perpetuate whiteness as they have been kidnapped into believing that whiteness steeped in subordination is what should be practiced and advanced in schools and society.

In addition, whiteness can be conceptualized as an "ideology of White supremacy that works through discourses" (Fylkesnes, 2018, p. 25). More than an individual act, action, practice, or behavior, whiteness is "deeply embedded in systems" (Sleeter, 2017, p. 165). Whiteness has become a "norm against which others are judged but also a powerful, if sometimes unconscious, justification for the status quo" (Castagno, 2013, p. 102). Thus, whiteness is about more than the bodies in which we were born; it is more than our physical characteristics. Whiteness is about how subjugation, supremacy, oppression, marginalization, harm, otherness, and conceptions of inferiority are practiced and carried out through actions. This book employs a dynamic way of thinking about whiteness and white practices that manifest through the behaviors of white (and other) bodies.

In this way, rather than white individuals feeling ostracized, unable to advance justice, or outside of the collective committed to racial justice, individuals across racial and ethnic backgrounds must be in the work of racial justice and the disruption of whiteness if we have a fighting chance to create the kinds of schools where racial minoritized students are honored, validated, and valued. Tanner (2019) stressed the need for whiteness to be addressed as a "complicated problem for white people" (p. 186). To be sure, rather than expecting and continuing to burden people of color to solve the challenges we face in education and society due to whiteness, it is a necessary responsibility of white communities to address whiteness. But whiteness has to also be addressed within communities and cultural practices of people who see whiteness as the sole way of existing in schools and society. In short, whiteness is less about what people embody as much as what they believe, know, understand, and practice. Whiteness is also about how white people flex their phenotype and their physically perceived dominance in the social world. And whiteness is about how people of color, albeit unintentionally and unawarely, adopt and embrace whiteness as a way to maintain an inequitable status quo. Whiteness contributes to anti-Black racism.

But What Is Anti-Black Racism?

Anti-Black racism takes racism to an even deeper, insidious level. The Black body is seen as a problem in the social world, and policies and practices are enacted to work against the spirit, mind, hopes, and dreams of Black people. Racism is so deeply ingrained in the fabric of U.S. society that Black people experience it across many confluent aspects of their lives. Dumas (2016) explained that

> antiblackness marks an irreconcilability between the Black and any sense of social or cultural regard. The aim of theorizing antiblackness is . . . to come to a deeper understanding of the Black condition within a context of utter contempt for, and acceptance of violence against the Black. (p. 13)

Anti-Black racism creates conditions, structures, and systems that almost guarantee outcomes that place Black people in the most precarious positions. To shed light on Dumas's (2016) insights regarding the contempt for and violence against the Black, Blackness, and the Black body, school punishment practices are often anti-Black. School grading policies and reward systems are often anti-Black. School dress code policies and expectations are often anti-Black. School curriculum practices are often anti-Black. School instructional practices are often anti-Black.

Florida's Department of Education decision to reject an Advanced Placement course covering African American Studies is an example of anti-Blackness on a systemic level. Stating that the course indoctrinates students to a political agenda suggests that there is something particularistic about a course in which students learn about Black people that would necessitate a kind of understanding and agenda contrary to the white-centric, colonized ways in which students experience other courses. Moreover, these inside-of-education anti-Black systems of racism are exacerbated by a serious movement in the United States to ensure the circumstances of Black children do not improve but worsen for them. As I am hopeful this book will be an educative tool to support leaders in building knowledge, attitudes, understanding, and insights about race, racism, whiteness, and anti-Black racism, Table 1.1 is designed to summarize major dimensions of constructs discussed throughout this book.

TABLE 1.1   Summarizing Race, Racism, Whiteness, and Anti-Black Racism

RACE	RACISM	WHITENESS	ANTI-BLACK RACISM
• Is much more than skin color. • Is one of the most difficult topics to discuss in education but one of the most important. • Is socially constructed. • Is historically constructed. • Is legally constructed. • Is phenotypically constructed. • Is geographically and spatially constructed. • Is often seen as a sociological imperative but should be considered in all aspects of curriculum, instruction, assessment, and relational practices.	• Occurs through power forces intentionally and unintentionally. • Is practiced through oppressive stereotypes, values, and beliefs deeply ingrained in society. • Is perpetuated through the prejudging of others based on explicit and implicit assumptions. • Is practiced by individuals who create structures and systems of racial injustice. • Results in a vicious cycle of violence, harm, trauma, and hurt of racial minoritized groups.	• Can be understood as a noun and a verb. • Is not only about white people but also concerns how all people act, behave, and move within and through society. • Is the norm against which others are compared. • Rejects, frowns on, and dehumanizes thoughts, beliefs, and practices that fall outside the white gaze. • Maintains an inequitable white status quo. • Indoctrinates white people into believing they are entitled to practicing white supremacy. • Creates a dominant lens in conceptualizing, prioritizing, and enacting curriculum, instruction, assessment, and relationship practices.	• Moves racism to an elevated level of hate for the Black body. • Advances deep contempt, harm, and disdain for Black people, their worldviews, and their practices. • Solidifies violence against the Black body through implicit and deeply ingrained hostility that is practiced and passed down through generational harm. • Intently studies any possible serious gains and improvement of Black communities in order to disrupt, distort, and end them by any means necessary.

Frontline Leadership

Having defined and conceptualized race, racism, whiteness, and anti-Black racism and their relevance throughout this book, I turn now to a discussion of the leadership I hope to advance in this book, Frontline Leadership. In most of this research outside and inside of education, Frontline Leadership is not well defined as a conceptual or analytic tool.

Frontline Leadership has been seen as a locale in the practices of organizations—the structural organizational hierarchy of first responders responsible for the vitality, health, and success of an organization. In education, Goldring and Sims (2005) wrote about the location of frontline leaders and queried "what people on the frontlines were actually thinking" (p. 234). Lee et al. (2022) studied the impact of a leadership program designed to help develop early career educators. In this way, Frontline Leadership has been conceptualized based on what people think and how leaders develop over time.

Frontline Leadership as a combined construct has been written about extensively in the health sciences. In the field of nursing, Jeavons's (2011) research focused on the role of organizations in supporting the development of next-generation nurses during times of uncertainty. Ohnmacht (2012) considered leaders and leadership in nursing and health care while Cherry (2014) stressed the necessity to learn from leadership practices on the frontlines under emergency and organizational complexities. Noordegraaf et al. (2016) examined professional and organizational logistics in developing essential tools for frontline medical leadership. In an industry study, Liu and McMurray (2004) researched the development of people working on the frontline, a shopfloor in the Australian automobile industry. Similarly, Block and Manning (2007) examined the "impact of a systemic approach to developing frontline leaders in a large Canadian healthcare organization" (p. 85). Locale—that is, frontline—was metaphorically used as the person or people in charge as well as the physical location of their work (such as the first people who interact with a person or issue).

Connecting frontline leaders to operational leaders, Noordegraaf et al. (2016) explained,

> In addition to learning new methods and techniques for diagnosing and treating patients, physicians become operational leaders or frontline leaders. They develop broader perspectives upon health-care delivery, see the provision of services as a more collaborative endeavor and deal with the tensions that are part of organizing health-care work. (p. 1113)

Thus, Frontline Leadership tells us something about methods and techniques necessary for powerful practices and organizational health care. Disciplines can learn from these methods and techniques across time, need, and space. Noordegraaf et al. (2016) explained,

> Becoming a frontline leader implies that (young) medical doctors develop a sense of organizing as well as organizational skills. They frame practical medical issues and problems as organizational problems that must not be ignored or reasoned away ("people above or around me will take care of it"), but coped with. This works in two ways. Some residents might discover that they are able to lead and manage health-care delivery. Other doctors might discover they have little affinity with leadership and management, but they might acknowledge the importance and difficulties of leading and managing service delivery. (p. 1131)

Conceptualizing the multidimensional aspects of the work of Frontline Leadership, Bunning (2000) wrote about four interrelated features. Bunning explained that while the four functions of Frontline Leadership may appear simplistic, actualizing these functions is extremely difficult for mostly trained clinicians without support in building organizational skills necessary for effective Frontline Leadership.

> [The four practices of Frontline Leadership], easily stated but difficult to fully implement, are required in order to fully develop the front-line leadership function. The practices are: implement a well-focused system of goals and feedback; employ rigorous leadership selection processes (including the removal of ineffective leaders); maintain well-developed and evolving human resource management systems; and implement training and development as an ongoing process. (p. 99)

Across these bodies of literature in education, health sciences, and industry, I identified several important commonalities regarding Frontline Leadership: (a) research tends to focus on the organizational hierarchical spaces of people (frontline work is outwardly facing while other locales are conceptualized more as behind-the-scenes work); (b) research tends to focus on developmental processes of people to merge their clinical knowledge and expertise with their capacity to learn, build, and practice organizational leadership skills; (c) research tends to conceptually center development of practices among people during what can be classified as complexity, challenges, and uncertainty; and (d) research tends to examine disconnects of practices and capacity to organize and lead to desired outcomes and effects.

Frontline Leadership in Education

Drawing from this established research, Frontline Leadership in education names, disrupts, addresses, and counters interconnected reality of oppression and human suffering that too many young people and adults experience in schools and society. Frontline leadership in education recognizes the backlash against the racial progress we were beginning to make in U.S. schools. This backlash is a direct reflection of the normative need for racism, whiteness, and anti-Black racism to remain firmly in place to ensure a status quo citizenry where white families continue to reap economic, social, environmental, health, educational, and other privileges and benefits while others suffer.

Frontline Leadership in education requires school leaders to move beyond mindsets, attitudes, dispositions, perceptions, beliefs, policies, and practices of white normalcy, where communities of color are not considered, are viewed as inconsequential, or are seen as problems in schools and society. Frontline Leadership in education moves beyond stale, dated, predetermined, irrelevant, underresponsive, disconnected, and "racially neutral" decision making that maintains a white-centric orientation to how the world works and how the world should work. Frontline Leadership in education is a leadership paradigm—a worldview about how to co-construct an ethos of healing, hope, possibility, and transformation where school leaders aggressively, deliberately, and persistently work to end punishment and pushout practices and amplify curriculum, instructional, assessment, and relational health in classrooms, schools, and districts (Morris, 2016).

> Frontline Leadership in education moves beyond stale, dated, predetermined, irrelevant, underresponsive, disconnected, and "racially neutral" decision making that maintains a white-centric orientation to how the world works and how the world should work.

Tenets of Frontline Leadership

From my vantage point and throughout this book, eight interrelated tenets shape what I am advancing as Frontline Leadership and practices of frontline leaders:

1.　Understand and Know the Research. *Frontline leaders immerse themselves in research about the intersections of teaching and learning about race, racism, whiteness, and anti-Black racism in schools and classrooms to advocate for justice.* As educators work through complex challenges and unsupportive policies and practices designed to distort, mask, mute, disguise, and eradicate the truth about societal and educational racism (and other forms of discrimination) in schools through the censorship and banning of curriculum and school practices, school leaders must be well-equipped and prepared to educate the masses about what research tells us about student learning and development and the kinds of practices educators must advance in schools to enact racial justice agendas.

2. Disrupt Color- and Race-Blindness. *Frontline leaders name, reject, call out, redirect, and disrupt color- and race-blindness in discussions, decision making, policy, and practice.* The work of race requires that leaders reject the idea that they are being fair, equitable, caring, and humanizing when they pretend to be color-blind or race-blind in their work. As frontline leaders, they facilitate the kinds of insights with educators to help them build tools to examine their own practices in a way that communicates that understanding the whole child (including the child's racial identity) complements how they will understand what is necessary to know, understand, and support student success. Moving away from stereotypes and negative preconceived notions, school leaders acknowledge systems of racial oppression and racism that students of color experience while building a school community that recognizes the many assets among these and all students. Instead, leaders help those in the community understand that adopting a color-blind orientation—where they claim to see only people and not race—contributes to inequitable and unjust practices and systems. In short, how can we co-design racially just spaces when we do not recognize the full humanity and identity of the students with whom we are working? Black students in mostly white spaces, for instance, often report that they feel invisible, not fully understood or accepted, and that their being Black is too often seen as a liability to their identity rather than an asset. Thus, to recognize racial injustice and work to disrupt it, we must "see," recognize, honor, build on, validate, confirm, and celebrate color and race.

3. Advocate Hard Work and Know Meritocracy as a Myth. *Frontline leaders understand meritocracy is a myth and cultivate a space of hard work while simultaneously acknowledging how success and achievement are shaped by generational systems of power.* Many white people believe that they have earned their positions, material wealth, and status inside and outside of education. However, white people must understand that their perceived success and status are not solely (or even mostly) a product of their own merit or hard work but instead a function of the ways in which broader systems have operated historically to place them in positions of success. Put simply, the curriculum is geared toward white students. Instructional practices are enacted to

white students' ways of seeing, understanding, experiencing, and interacting with the world of learning. Relational practices tend to be guided by white norms and interactions. Assessment practices tend to promote competition and individual success, and do not build on the many strengths of students of color. Collectively, in schools, if young people believe their success and achievements are solely functions of their individual efforts, intellect, or capacity without understanding how educational practices are designed for white students and to maintain white norms of excellence, vis-à-vis whiteness, students of color may start to believe the lie that they are somehow inherently cognitively inferior to white students. White students benefit not only from their merit but also from structural racism and a history of oppressing minoritized communities. Their privileges are stubbornly in place and have been (and will be) passed down infinitely through the generations. Recognizing, naming, and acknowledging meritocracy is a myth does not mean that white people do not and should not work hard. To the contrary, young white people work hard and should be encouraged to put forth their best efforts at succeeding even beyond their current situations. At the same time, white people must also understand that they have a cumulative advantage over others because the playing field is far from level in districts, schools, classrooms, worlds of education, work, and life.

> Instructional practices are enacted to white students' ways of seeing, understanding, experiencing, and interacting with the world of learning.

4. Move Beyond Abstractions of Race, Racism, Anti-Black Racism, and Whiteness. *Frontline leaders encourage and facilitate understanding and engagement of structural forms of racial oppression while documenting and showcasing how individuals make systems that (must) influence change.* Because racism and other dimensions of racial oppression are often discussed through the lenses and frames of structures, institutions, and systems, educators may believe they are fighting an impossible battle because of the abstractness of the role of individuals in these systems. White students (and their families) may be well-intentioned, have nonwhite friends, and engage in community service. However, they may not understand that racial injustice and structural discrimination are functions of how the overwhelming number of decision makers are white in, for instance, institutions, positions, and structures that are at the foundation of structural oppression, which may lead to inequitable hiring practices, lending patterns, school and district funding and zoning, as well as curriculum and assessment practices. Thus, if

leaders only read about, focus on, talk about, and build tools to address racism as a structural oppression, white people may fail to see how they are actors, enactors, perpetuators, contributors, and reinforcers of racism, whiteness, and anti-Black racism. In this way, interrogating the role of the individual in building systems and structures of racism is essential in Frontline Leadership.

5. Reject Racial Neutrality. *Frontline leaders view neutrality as a disposition of racial injustice, and they are forthcoming, forthright, and deliberate about their commitment to racial justice and racial equity.* Leaders must not hide in the background and just hope their colleagues and young people will engage in the work of racial justice and racial equity through neutrality. Such leadership helps communities understand that their neutrality is a form of complacency, acceptance of racism, perpetuation of anti-Black racism, and support of a racist social order that will continue to marginalize racially minoritized communities. Frontline leaders help others understand how neutrality, apathy, and indifference are positions of injustice that lead to inequitable policies and practices. In short, those in a school community are working either *toward* racial (and other forms of) justice or *against* it. I have heard students of color talk about how disappointed they were when white people (teachers, families, and students) they trusted the most did not show up for them and speak out when they had experienced racism. Many of these white people, who had been kind and otherwise supportive of students of color, retreated to spaces of neutrality when issues of racism and racial injustice were presented and they needed to speak up and speak out. These teachers claim that they do not want to be "political" and that they do not want to create tension and separation between themselves and their colleagues, white students, or white parents and families. In order to work against psychologically damaging environments, school leaders co-create spaces where all interrogate the ways in which racial neutrality is a position of injustice.

> I have heard students of color talk about how disappointed they were when white people (teachers, families, and students) they trusted the most did not show up for them and speak out when they had experienced racism.

6. Learn and Develop Every Day. *Frontline leaders recognize and embrace the reality that they are not all-knowing, and so they work in community with others in co-planning and co-designing a racially just community for scalable improvement.* Leaders examine the best of themselves, amplify their assets, try to improve areas of challenge, and co-construct a community of educators, staff, broader community members, policymakers, and young

people in the fight for racially affirming environments. In this way, leaders are increasing their capacity to improve their own practices while they simultaneously plan, design, and support the learning and development of others. School leaders must develop leadership capacity to co-construct, co-design, and co-plan an educational ethos that pulls people and communities together rather than pushing them further apart. This means that multiple perspectives, ideas, and insights can be interrogated in the best interest of those in the learning environment.

> School leaders must develop leadership capacity to co-construct, co-design, and co-plan an educational ethos that pulls people and communities together rather than pushing them further apart.

7. Revise Punishment Practices and Decrease Pushout. *Frontline leaders are resolute in their learning about and advancing the reality that pushout and punishment policies tend to undermine racial justice.* Leaders understand that one of the most pervasive and central issues they must constantly address is the conflation of punishment and disciplinary practices where an overwhelmingly high proportion of office referrals, suspensions, and expulsions are for students of color. School leaders work to build disciplinary practices, think outside of traditional punishment practices that exclude students, and commit to the development of curricular, instructional, relational, and assessment practices that recognize and amplify student inclusion, student assets, student potential, student needs, student identity, and student psychological and mental wellness. Such educators unapologetically disrupt individual and intersecting dimensions of racism, sexism, homophobia, xenophobia, and other forms of oppression in their classrooms, schools, districts, states, and nations and disrupt pushout practices that reify stereotypes that continue to maintain whiteness as normative behavior in classrooms and schools.

8. Involve and Center Young People. Perhaps most importantly, *Frontline Leadership involves voices, perspectives, insights, and recommendations of young people in racial justice work.* School leaders and educators conceptualize, plan, and execute racial justice work with young people. Racial justice and equity work— work planned and designed to disrupt racism, whiteness, and anti-Black racism—cannot be well and effectively executed and enacted without involving young people. School leaders recognize that in order to cultivate humanizing, transformative, and racially just communities, young people's insights, paradigms, commitments, and, consequently, practices must be prominently involved in the planning, designing, and enacting of racial justice work.

TABLE 1.2   Tenets of Frontline Leadership

FRONTLINE LEADERSHIP TENETS	RATIONALE AND DESCRIPTIONS
Understand and Know the Research	Leaders must know the science to advocate for and support their educator colleagues and young people as they navigate backlash against truth.
Disrupt Color- and Race-Blindness	Leaders move beyond color- and race-blindness—they play the race card—to infuse racially humanizing discussions, decision making, policy, and practice.
Advocate Hard Work and Know Meritocracy as a Myth	Leaders cultivate a community where people work hard but understand that success comes from factors outside of ability, effort, intellect, and merit.
Move Beyond Abstractions of Race, Racism, Anti-Black Racism, and Whiteness	Leaders help educators understand their individual role in improving structures and systems. Individuals make systems of race, racism, anti-Black racism, and whiteness. Leaders provide concrete accessible language and examples to help others know and do more to disrupt racism, whiteness, and anti-Black racism.
Reject Racial Neutrality	Leaders expect and support educators to always work toward equity and justice and move beyond positions of racial apathy and centrism.
Learn and Develop Every Day	Leaders consistently work to build dynamic teams of expertise and reject the idea that they are all-knowing or that their learning is fixed and static.
Revise Punishment Practices and Decrease Pushout	Leaders focus on building communities of discipline over punishment while rejecting pushout practices and promoting communities of inclusion that honor individual and community assets and diversity.
Involve and Center Young People	Leaders understand and advance the reality that true racial justice work can never be accomplished without the deep commitment and involvement of young people.

Pressing toward and actualizing these tenets and features of Frontline Leadership for racial justice as captured in Table 1.2 are importantly a function of school leaders' thinking, mindsets, dispositions, paradigms, philosophies, and beliefs that will shape their practices.

So much of the work of good leadership is understanding *why* outcomes, outputs, structures, systems, tools, experiences, and interactions are *what* they are. In other words, Frontline Leadership requires deep levels of self, school, community, policy, and practice examination to transform, reform, and improve conditions in which we live and learn. Where the work of racial justice is concerned, I have observed that too many school leaders, policymakers, and others tinker around the margins and edges of equity and justice. They do not know how to, or they are not committed to, building a repository and toolkit to actually develop practices to do more than treat the real illness of racism, anti-Black racism, and whiteness. Rather than eradicating the root cause of the illness, school leaders continue to implement and advocate for practices that work for the white majority, and students of color are made to conform, assimilate, get in line, or suffer. Advancing deep moral commitments, Frontline Leadership requires a deep and sustained paradigm shift to what leadership is in schools and what it *should* be.

Frontline leaders address and attempt to cure the underlying conditions of racism (attempts to subordinate, disenfranchise, and dehumanize individuals and collectives of people), whiteness (the practice of perpetuating a normative white way of living and being for white supremacy), and anti-Black racism (deeply ingrained disdain for Black people that pushes above and beyond general forms of racism such that, for Black people, racism alone is insufficient, so added levels of hate, subjugation, and violence must be practiced on the Black body).

An important charge of *The Race Card: Leading the Fight for Truth in America's Schools* is to bring to the consciousness of leaders the many ways in which they (may) contribute to the dysfunction of districts, schools, and classrooms throughout the United States. An explicit focus on truth-knowing, truth-understanding, and truth-telling, in the next section, I discuss central aspects of healing and curing that must take place through Frontline Leadership to disrupt and address racism, whiteness, and anti-Black racism. To understand what is true and necessary to heal and cure racial injustice, we must understand the many lies that frame, perpetuate, and advance the conditions of racism and discrimination in schools and communities.

Healing and Curing Under(Lie)ing Conditions

Frontline leaders *must address and work to heal and cure what I am calling the under(Lie)ing conditions we face maintaining race, whiteness, and anti-Black racism in America, historically and contemporarily.* If school leaders are not co-creating environments that overtly work to address untruths, lies about race, racism, and anti-Black racism that are pervasive in schools and society, we will not see the kinds of progress necessary to stop the harm, hurt, violence, marginalization, othering, and traumatizing that communities of color experience through schooling practices.

> If we have a fighting chance at making the world a better, more socially and racially just place, it will take the work of those in schools to impact the broader society.

It is important to note that I am including society in my discussion about what is essential to consider among school leaders and school leadership. If we have a fighting chance at making the world a better, more socially and racially just place, it will take the work of those in schools to impact broader society.

Figure 1.1 is designed for school leaders to study and map the complexities of the issues we face in education broadly (macro) as well as specifically (micro). Rather than considering these issues independent of race, school leaders are invited to think about the ways in which racism, whiteness, and anti-Black racism perpetuate and undermine progress forward. From where do people *lead* in addressing the many needs, challenges, and opportunities we face in education to heal under(Lie)ing conditions we face in schools and society? Frontline Leadership requires deep, developing, iterative, and robust knowledge, understanding, and explicit attention to addressing the lies that result in potentially devastating outcomes for racially minoritized communities.

- *Under(Lie)ing Condition:* **Pushout Lie**

  Schools believe if they push minoritized students out of classrooms, over refer them to the office to punish them for "misbehavior," then student behavior improves, and they learn more.

  Potential Outcomes and Opportunity Gaps:

  Missed instructional time; disproportionate suspensions and expulsions; cradle-to-school-to-prison intersection.

- *Under(Lie)ing Condition:* **Representation Lie**

  Schools believe, support, and advance the idea that science, technology, engineering, and mathematics (STEM) success and participation are a function and result of innate ability and skill (McGee, 2021). This representation lie would adopt the idea that schools do not and cannot play a role in addressing the underrepresentation and under-enrollment of Black and Brown students in STEM areas, particularly in middle and high school, because they believe it is too late for these students to participate and take advantage of STEM courses and experiences.

  Potential Outcomes and Opportunity Gaps:

  Fewer STEM-related learning opportunities for minoritized students; Black and Brown students do not see themselves as "STEM people"; STEM pipeline is deeply affected; and minoritized students move into non-STEM-related majors and careers.

- *Under(Lie)ing Condition:* **Advanced Placement Lie**

  Schools do not guide, shepherd, recommend, or encourage racially minoritized students into advanced classes or prestigious and elite clubs and organizations because they do not believe this work is central to their jobs and mission. Schools believe it is acceptable that students of color are celebrated only or mostly in "big-time" sport and not expected to be well represented in white-dominated spaces, such as gifted and talented programs, BETA clubs, quiz bowl teams, and so forth (Ford, 2021).

Potential Outcomes and Opportunity Gaps:

Rigorous learning experiences, opportunities, and exposure are designed for students who are socially constructed as "smart," "capable," or "deserving." Students of color begin to internalize the lie that they somehow are not deserving or worthy of these "extra-" or co-curricular opportunities.

- *Under(Lie)ing Condition:* **Collaboration and Partnership Lie**

Educators in schools believe they are the best, most informed arbiters of knowledge and knowing in a school and district. Educators build poor collaborations and partnerships between schools and families and communities of color they serve because they see families of their students as deficient, unintelligent, uncaring, deficit, and not capable of contributing to the excellence of school or community.

Potential Outcomes and Opportunity Gaps:

Families, parents, and communities do not trust schools to teach, support, and nurture their children. Unnecessary barriers and tensions keep families and communities from working together to support the learning and development of young people.

- *Under(Lie)ing Condition:* **Recruitment Lie**

Schools do not deliberately, assertively, consciously, and relentlessly build recruitment and retention strategies to increase the number of effective teachers of color because they believe these teachers do not exist (Kohli, 2021). Schools practice the same recruitment strategies for teachers of color as they do for white educators and believe they will be able to increase the teacher of color pipeline and representation.

Potential Outcomes and Opportunity Gaps:

Low (and declining) numbers of teachers of color in the teaching force; fewer teachers of color as curriculum, instructional, assessment, and relational experts and mentors; fewer teachers of color in the pipeline capable of transitioning into school leadership.

- *Under(Lie)ing Condition:* **Model Minority Lie**

Schools believe that all Asian American students have the same ethnic origin and are a monolith. Schools essentialize Asian

American students as a "model" minority and work to make them believe they are better than other communities of color. Schools believe Asian American students are not negatively affected by teasing or stereotyping.

Potential Outcomes and Opportunity Gaps:

Asian American students feel stuck between school communities that do not honor and understand them and are pressured to live up to myths about identities, heritage, ethnic origins, achievement, and socialization as models. Diverse ethnic origins are erased. Asian American students are blamed for and/or teased about "bird flu" and/or "China virus"; these types of interactions are embarrassing, dehumanizing, and stressful.

- *Under(Lie)ing Condition:* **Mental and Psychological Health Lie**

Schools believe mental health challenges should be handled outside of the school building and do not put resources into building a community that promotes mental, emotional, and psychological health of educators and young people.

Potential Outcome and Opportunity Gaps:

Educators and young people are forced to work through traumatic experiences without support. Educators and young people's toxic behaviors are punished as irrational and disconnected from their mental and psychological wellness.

- *Under(Lie)ing Condition:* **Avoidance Lie**

Schools believe they must be silent, evasive, and unconcerned about political discourse against the teaching of the truth in schools. School leaders and others believe their jobs can be and are apolitical and do not understand how their beliefs, values, and actions are political, politically charged, and politically received. School educators believe they can be apolitical and can avoid discourses about the truth in their work.

Potential Outcomes and Opportunity Gaps:

Educators are afraid to teach for fear of losing their positions. Young people may internalize the idea that political bullies win based on lies if they scream loud enough. Young people do not experience the courage, advocacy, and commitment of their educators to fight for truth as they learn about historical and contemporary racist structures, institutions, doctrines, policies, insights, and practices meant to maintain an inequitable, "politically neutral," status quo.

- *Under(Lie)ing Condition:* **Curriculum Narrowing Lie**

Schools believe that they should (and must) narrow the curriculum that pushes out the arts and physical education, especially in "high-need" schools. Schools believe that they can somehow make up for two years of pandemic "missed" learning opportunities and advance the idea that schools should focus on trying to get their students to make up for the missed time at school in standardized testing areas to the exclusion of other subjects.

Potential Outcomes and Opportunity Gaps:

Young people miss opportunities to learn and experience a broader curriculum that addresses the imagination, aesthetics, mobility, and physical wellness. Stress is intensified for educators, families, communities, parents, and young people as they are fixated on what learning opportunities were missed during the pandemic rather than a centralized focus on what young people, communities, and educators actually learned and benefited from across subject areas, including the arts.

- *Under(Lie)ing Condition:* **Language Lie**

Schools see language as arbitrary and inconsequential. Schools misrepresent gaps in student test scores as achievement gaps. Schools believe the onus of test scores and student outcomes are a function and result of student effort and mask the negative results as achievement gaps instead of opportunity gaps.

Potential Outcomes and Opportunity Gaps:

Opportunity gaps across disciplines are masked in the language of achievement gaps. The onus for low student success is placed on students and their families. Schools pretend that the language usage is irrelevant to the situations and circumstances we face in education.

- *Under(Lie)ing Condition:* **Censorship Lie**

Schools ignore, ostracize, minimize, censor, silence, and distort developmentally appropriate curriculum and learning opportunities and intersections of race and racism because they believe it will somehow indoctrinate students into a particular identity or promote anti-patriotism.

Potential Outcomes and Opportunity Gaps:

Students are marginalized. Students feel disconnected, unheard, and unwelcomed in schools and districts. Students of color are underserved because of confounding marginalization they experience due to their race and other identity markers. Students are taught one-dimensional histories that tell only one side of a story. Racist history and conditions are at jeopardy of repeating themselves because they are not addressed, talked about, critiqued, nuanced, and understood.

- *Under(Lie)ing Condition:* **Equal Funding Lie**

  Districts and policymakers believe they should pursue and adopt equal funding and resource mechanisms rather than equitable ones that allocate more resources to historically underserved school communities, where there is a strong majority of young people of color.

  Potential Outcomes and Opportunity Gaps:

  Schools and communities that need the most resources are punished through a framework of equality (at best), and inequity is misunderstood and accelerated as the right framework to pursue.

Many of the processes, mechanisms, and under(Lie)ing conditions in the previous bulleted paragraphs have been in place for years, and frontline leaders must confront these lies. Even when educators, including school leaders, claim to be anti-racist and fully committed to the full range of diversity among their students, their practices suggest otherwise, as the processes and mechanisms in place and carried forward result in potential *outcomes* and *opportunity gaps* that do more harm than good. The interrelated issues are a result of unacknowledged, unresolved, and increasingly underexplored under(Lie)ing conditions that do not address root causes of systemic injustice, harm, violence, injustice, and inequity.

As a result, frontline leaders must work to co-construct healing processes that disrupt inequitable outcomes that have become so deeply ingrained and normalized in the fabric of America's educational systems, schooling, and broader society. The processes and outcomes previously discussed are broad, diverse, and yet interconnected. And each of these processes and outcomes negatively impacts communities of color. Thus, until we get real about racism, whiteness, and anti-Black racism, and stop being dishonest—that is, stop lying about the ways in which racism in America and our schools are still stubbornly pervasive—our nation's schools (and society) will not heal. To be clear, where healing, disrupting, and address-ing racism, whiteness, and anti-Black racism are concerned, society will not significantly improve unless schools do. A discursive and dialogic endeavor, young people in schools give us our best chance at working to make society and the broader world a more civil and socially just place. In Table 1.3, I summarize what I have conceptualized as under(lie)ing conditions that Frontline Leadership must address for truth.

TABLE 1.3   Under(Lie)ing Conditions and Potential Opportunity Gaps

UNDER(LIE)ING CONDITIONS	POTENTIAL OUTCOMES AND OPPORTUNITY GAPS
Pushout Lie: Schools believe if they push minoritized students out of classrooms, over refer them to the office to punish them for "misbehavior," then student behavior will improve and students will learn more.	• Missed instructional time • Disproportionate suspensions and expulsions • Cradle-to-school-to-prison intersection
Representation Lie: Schools believe, support, and advance the idea that science, technology, engineering, and mathematics (STEM) success and participation is a function and result of innate ability and skill. Schools do not and cannot play a role in adding to the underrepresentation and under-enrollment of Black and Brown students in STEM areas.	• Fewer STEM-related learning opportunities for minoritized bodies • Black (and some Brown) students do not see themselves as "STEM people." • STEM pipeline is deeply affected, and minoritized bodies move into non-STEM-related majors and careers.
Advanced Placement Lie: Schools do not guide, shepherd, or encourage minoritized students into enrolling or joining advanced classes, clubs, and organizations. Schools believe it is acceptable that students of color are celebrated only or mostly in "big-time" sport and not expected to be well represented in white-dominated spaces such as gifted and talented programs, BETA clubs, quiz bowl teams, and so forth.	• Lack of experience, learning, and contributions through experiences designed for students who are socially constructed as "smart," "capable," or "deserving" of these courses and organizations • Students of color begin to internalize the lie that they somehow are not deserving or worthy of these "extra-" or co-curricular opportunities.
Collaboration and Partnership Lie: Educators in schools believe they are the best, most informed arbiters of knowledge and knowing in a school and district. Schools build poor collaborations and partnerships between schools and the families and communities they serve because they see the families of their students as deficient and not capable of contributing to the excellence of school or community.	• Families, parents, and communities do not trust schools to teach, support, and nurture their children. • Unnecessary barriers and tensions keep families and communities from working together to support the learning and development of young people.
Recruitment Lie: Schools do not assertively build recruitment and retention strategies to increase the number of high-quality, effective teachers of color because they believe these teachers do not exist. Schools believe if they practice the same recruiting strategies across the board as they recruit teachers of color, they will yield a strong teacher of color cadre in districts and schools.	• Low (and declining) numbers of teachers of color in the teaching force • Fewer teachers of color as mentors and curriculum engineers
Model Minority Lie: Schools believe that all Asian American students have the same ethnic origin and are a monolith. Schools essentialize Asian American students as a "model" minority and work to make them believe they are better than other communities of color. Schools do not	• Asian American students feel stuck between school communities that do not honor and understand them and are pressured to live up to myths about identities, heritage, ethnic origins, achievement, and socialization as models.

(Continued)

(Continued)

UNDER(LIE)ING CONDITIONS	POTENTIAL OUTCOMES AND OPPORTUNITY GAPS
believe that broader disturbing discourses about Asian American communities affect these students' sense of belonging and self-worth.	• Diverse ethnic origins are erased. • Asian American students are blamed for and/or teased about "bird flu" and/or "China virus"; such interactions are embarrassing, dehumanizing, and stressful.
Mental and Psychological Health Lie: Schools believe mental health challenges should be handled outside of the school building and do not put resources into building a community that promotes the mental, emotional, and psychological health of educators and young people.	• Educators and young people must work through traumatic experiences without support. • Educators and young people's toxic behaviors are punished as irrational and disconnected from their mental and psychological wellness.
Avoidance Lie: Schools believe they must be silent, evasive, and unconcerned about political discourse against the teaching and leadership of truth in schools.	• Educators are afraid to teach and lead for fear of losing their positions. • Young people may internalize the idea that political bullies win based on lies if they scream loud enough. • Young people do not experience the courage, advocacy, and commitment of their educators to fight for truth as they learn about historical and contemporary racist structures, institutions, doctrines, policies, insights, and practices meant to maintain an inequitable status quo.
Curriculum Narrowing Lie: Schools believe they should (and must) narrow the curriculum that pushes out the arts and physical education, especially in "high-need" schools.	• Young people miss opportunities to learn and experience a broader curriculum that addresses the imagination, aesthetics, and mobility.
Language Lie: Schools see language as arbitrary and inconsequential. Schools misrepresent gaps in student test scores as achievement gaps. Schools believe the onus of test scores and student outcomes are a function and result of student effort and mask the negative results as achievement gaps instead of opportunity gaps.	• Opportunity gaps across disciplines are masked in the language of achievement gaps. • Onus for low student success is placed on students and their families.
Censorship Lie: Schools ignore, ostracize, minimize, censor, silence, and distort developmentally appropriate curriculum and learning opportunities and intersections of race and racism.	• Marginalization of students • Students feel disconnected, unheard, and unwelcomed in schools and districts. • Students of color are underserved because of confounding marginalizing they experience due to their race and other identity markers.
Equal Funding Lie: Districts and policymakers believe they should pursue and adopt equal funding and resource mechanisms rather than equitable ones that allocate more resources to historically underserved school communities where there is a majority of young people of color.	• Schools and communities that need the most resources are punished through a framework of equality (at best), and inequity is perpetuated and accelerated.

Chief among the issues frontline leaders face are conflicts and tensions about what can and should be taught in schools within and across the United States. What role must school leaders play in navigating and negotiating curriculum and pedagogical practices in schools? Proliferating tensions about teaching and learning about race in schools begs the question: Are we approaching a race war in America, or are we experiencing a race war already?

Race War

Are we amid a race war in the United States? If we are not, recent occurrences in America would certainly suggest we are potentially approaching a race war. I will elaborate throughout this book on why I believe we are in danger of a race war within the United States and *the role school leaders must play* in classrooms, schools, and districts to arm educators and young people with tools they need to fight for truth and disrupt racism, whiteness, anti-Black racism, and other forms of discrimination both within traditional school buildings and beyond. Leadership is difficult. Frontline Leadership during this moment and movement of racial divisiveness in schools and society is even more challenging. While I lay out many intersecting challenges we face in education and society, this book is about supporting educational leaders in co-creating spaces where communities come together to make society better: *lead for truth, support educators as they teach truth, and push back against policies designed to perpetuate and reify lies.* I argue that without the fortitude of leaders and leadership in this moment we are headed toward a race war—a civil war within the United States that will potentially regress racial progress, setting us back as a nation to pre–civil rights times.

I argue that without the fortitude of leaders and leadership in this moment that we are headed toward a race war—a civil war within the United States that will potentially regress racial progress, setting us back as a nation to pre–civil rights times.

This book is both frank about racial and racist social ills of this nation and society and concurrently optimistic about opportunity structures and what it will take for our nation to come together and either prevent a race war or work to calm it. Thus, this is a book about how manifestations of racism (historically, contemporarily, and before us) have been an integral part of our school system in the United States, and the book is also about why *educational leaders must learn from and work with community* to address the reality that schooling systems and processes were not designed for communities of color. Understanding the role of schools and education gives us our best chance of knowing about and addressing the race war.

Although ripe with serious under(Lie)ing conditions, scars, and strife, we must admit that race and racism have improved in America over time. This fact that we have seen some progress regarding structural racism is an important data point for the important work that must be done moving forward.

Frontline leaders must remind young people and educators that progress can be made as we have in the past and that we can and must *pursue* an end to racism, whiteness, and anti-Black racism. However, as Bell (1980) and the critical race theory movement have reminded us, progress forward for racial justice is often slow and at the pace of those in power. Thus, Frontline Leadership must be deliberate, careful, and urgent. Young people who are hurt most cannot wait on policies and practices of truth.

> Frontline Leadership must be deliberate, careful, and urgent.

Young people cannot wait on developing tools to fight the race war. Educators, working in collaboration and partnership with young people, families, policymakers, and broader communities, played a meteoric role in the recent racial progress we have made. For instance, at least in response to one of the most horrific situations we observed as a nation in the killing of George Floyd, in 2020, we witnessed this nation pause, although only for a short time, to say something and potentially do something about racism and the structural toxicity emanating from it. In a very few occasions, the nation did something to disrupt the persistent and pervasive racism, whiteness, and anti-Black racism plaguing this country.

We witnessed overt dialogues about racism in schools and beyond. We observed schools working with partners, including university researchers, to learn more about developing and implementing research-based racially inclusive policies and practices. Although these efforts were short lived, institutions, organizations, and individuals (from small church groups to neighborhood gatherings) pushed forward agendas to learn more about what in this world was happening to bring us to a place where such a murder could occur, where police officer Chauvin positioned his knee on the neck of unarmed and under-responsive George Floyd's neck until all the breath left Floyd's body.

Quickly, fueled by racist and separatist politics, efforts to talk about and engage with each other to address and build policies and practices to counter racial injustice were halted. Tensions began to mount because, in my view, our nation was taking another major step forward toward racial justice. These major steps ahead, although slow in progress and nowhere near what is necessary to end racism, whiteness, and anti-Black racism, are excellent examples of what can happen when the center of our work and lives are for equity and justice for all. We saw, for instance, major discussions about racial injustice with the murder of Emmett Till. We saw major steps forward toward racial justice with the killing of Martin Luther King Jr., to a lesser degree Malcolm X, and even with the police attacks on Rodney King. In this way, America can get better as a nation. However, why does it take such horrific violence against Black bodies for progress to be made? Why is the progress so slow and unsteady? Why does the progress last for such short periods of time before resolutory protests and race wars begin? And why is it so hard for progress forward to be made when the violence, hurt, harm, and dehumanization occurs with Black women?

> Why does it take such horrific violence against Black bodies for progress to be made?

The optimistic spirit of this book is dedicated to historical evidence of racial progress that I hope frontline leaders will embrace as what can and must be done to address the race war in the United States, communities, schools, and classrooms. In light of the racial progress we made in the past, we can make progress again even in the midst of polarizing attempts to separate us from truth, justice, democracy, possibility, opportunity, and healing. But rather than moving forward at a snail's speed while the bodies, minds, and experiences of people are color are affronted daily, frontline leaders understand the importance and urgency of now.

The Urgency of Now: A Pace Imperative

This book is meant to help school leaders *now*—in this moment—those new to leadership roles and those more seasoned. *The word* now *is meant to signal a moment of urgency (now) as well as a sense of the times in which we are living (now) where there is tremendous backlash against people, projects, products, and events meant to move us closer to a racially just democracy in the United States.* The book is meant to encourage and support educators to keep pressing and keep fighting during these times of unprecedented uncertainty. Young people need, deserve, and should expect our unwavering courage, confidence, truth-telling, and modeling of leadership during these times of polarizing politics, harmful practices, and traumatizing effects of racism.

Leadership *now* means we are, in the words of James Baldwin, willing to "go for broke" in the fight for what we know to be necessary to make schools places where young people—all of them—feel safe, are psychologically and mentally healthy, and know they belong because they bring their full beings into the learning environment.

Change is often at the moderately slow pace of those in power. For example, Lopez (2003) wrote, "Racism always remains firmly in place but that social progress advances at the pace that White people determine is reasonable and judicious" (p. 84). Change is often *purposefully method-ically,* and *skillfully* slow and at the will and design of those who make decisions for communities that are often not at the table of power. Ladson-Billings (1999) explained,

> The traditional chronicle of U.S. history records a story of forward moving progress, no matter how slow. Issues such as voting rights for African Americans and women, school desegregation, and social desegregation of public accommodations unfolded at a very slow pace. (p. 232)

According to Bell (1980), white people may support social jus-tice and equity-oriented policies and practices yet still believe that injustice can be "remedied effectively without altering the status of whites" (p. 522). This fallacy—that white people can (and should) maintain their privileges without making changes—is what hurts young people in education. Castagno and Lee (2007, p. 4) explained that those in the majority will advance social justice agendas "when such advances suit" their own self-interests. The point is that peo-ple in power are sometimes, in theory and rhetoric, supportive of policies and practices that do not oppress and discriminate against others as long as they (those in power) do not have to alter their own ways and systems, statuses, and privileges of experiencing life. Lopez (2003) maintained that interest convergence centralizes "the belief that Whites will tolerate and advance the interests of people of color only when they *promote the self-interests of Whites*" (p. 84; emphasis added).

Frontline Leadership requires an insistence on the posing of questions among those in a learning environment such as the following:

- What privileges am I willing to give up as we co-create this context in a more racially just way for people of color?

- How do my own self-interests overshadow the collective good?

In many ways, again, I believe our most promising population for build-ing a more just society is through the fortitude, insights, and leader-ship of young people. So, leaders must tap into the leadership genius, interests, potentials, and capacities of young people in their work for racial justice. This means that the preceding questions require the self-reflection of young people, just as adults are thinking through the ways in which interests of power supersede and overshadow those of justice and equity. Young people tend to be ready to move our lives and work forward for a more just world (Milner, 2015). *Adults, quite often, are those who struggle the most with advancing racial justice because of their racist historical views and values, implicit biases, dangerous politics, self-interests over collective ones, and desire to maintain a racist, inequitable world.* So, young people must be active participants in our work for racial justice in schools and society. Helping young people understand their own privileges and the ways in which their own actions (and inactions) can be used to ignore, contribute to, or disrupt racial justice is a charge that frontline leaders understand, embrace, and cultivate. With young people at the center, we can get better as a nation and do so much faster than a pace imperative that keeps situations firmly in place over time. The work of building racially just-minded young people is not trivial, and recommendations on how to cultivate young people's work in this area will be addressed throughout this book. Frontline Leadership *now* requires that school leaders are not neutral, agnostic, elusive, or evasive about the potentially harmful effects that racism contributes to the human condition.

> Our most promising population for building a more just society is through the fortitude, insights, and leadership of young people.

To be sure, in the context of education, frontline leaders play an extraordinarily important role in our work to help young people build knowledge, attitudes, dispositions, mindsets, worldviews, habits, skills, and practices necessary to live in an increasingly racially (and overall) diverse classroom, district, school, community, nation, and world. *My point in this book is certainly not that people must or should all have the same beliefs, worldviews, or practices on topics of racial justice and equity.* On the contrary, our experiences warrant, and our pursuit of a truly democratic nation-state demands, variation in how we see and interact with the world. However, because polarizing views about humanity, human worth, human potential, human contributions, as well as *who* and *what* matters in our society are at odds, Frontline Leadership must be centrally involved in the necessary work of helping young people build informed decisions as they learn, live, and hopefully positively impact and improve the world. Otherwise, if we are not keenly and astutely addressing racism, whiteness, and anti-Black racism now, we will continue to witness the effects and outcomes of under(Lie)ing conditions gone unresolved, such as:

- The alarming and disproportionate number of deaths of Black and Brown people from COVID-19

- Police shootings and murders of Black bodies such as Breonna Taylor, George Floyd, Ahmaud Arbery, Rekia Boyd, and Antwon Rose Jr.

- Backlash to Colin Kaepernick for his refusal to stand during the U.S. national anthem

- Ongoing national immigration debates over children being taken from their families and placed in fenced cages

- The Flint, Michigan, and Jackson, Mississippi, contaminated water crises with highly disproportionate communities of color

- The brutal shooting of nine parishioners in a church in Charleston, South Carolina

Indeed, although people may develop varying views on topics that are controversial and consequential, we should all be able to engage with each other in civil, humanizing, restorative, and anti-racist ways. Frontline leaders create the conditions by which this engagement is possible.

About Readers of This Book

The Race Card: Leading the Fight for Truth in America's Schools is a book for school leaders who will come to see themselves or at least aspects of their leadership as frontline. The book is written for both those in school leadership programs preparing to become leaders and those early and more seasoned in their careers as school leaders. I am conceptualizing leadership as broader than a building school principal although many of the recommendations and insights herein are applicable to the principal. As a former classroom teacher and one who has studied the practices of many classroom teachers, I know that classroom educators are and can be leaders and might learn from this book, particularly if they aspire to move into broader (than the classroom) spaces of leadership.

School counselors, social workers, psychologists, and psychiatrists may find important lessons for their role and leadership work throughout this book as I focus on the importance of understanding and co-creating mentally, emotionally, and psychologically safe social contexts. For sure, assistant and associate principals will learn from this book as there is an explicit focus on the role of curriculum engineering, instructional innovation, assessment realignment and relevance, relationship cultivation, and reimagining pushout and punishment practices in schools and classrooms. Frontline leaders set the stage for powerful, transformative, and racially just curriculum, instruction, assessment, and relationships in schools. Notably, this book is written so that young people, high school students in particular, might read and engage with the text. To be sure, young people should be part of the reading, thinking, nuancing, challenging, reconceptualizing, and discourses about them in our press toward ending racism, whiteness, and anti-Black racism.

I distinguish throughout this book between leaders and leadership. Leaders in this work occupy the bodies, that is, the vessels, that enact the kinds of practices we need in education through Frontline Leadership. Thus, I focus on the role of leaders in leadership throughout this book. What I have learned is that *our feelings* (affective) and *our thoughts, conceptions, mindsets, paradigms, and beliefs* (cognitive) about what is important in anti-racism work manifest in *what we do and how we act on realities* (behavior).

I have learned that some people of color, unfortunately, subscribe to, embrace, and reify whiteness because, for example, they (a) have had some material, academic, societal, professional, career, and normative success; (b) fail to empathize with those from under-resourced communities and who have not benefited from the privileges; or (c) accept a meritocratic way of functioning in the world. Further, because of their own personal success, perhaps their educational attainment, the type of home they live in, the school their children attend, and their financial or other material possessions, they may believe that they are superior to other people of color (Milner, 2015, 2020b). Moreover, some Black people may have deeply ingrained self-hate for the Black community. Indeed, no one group of people is monolithic, and diversity within a racial group is necessary and forward thinking. Black people may have similar lived experiences, but their interpretations of, resilience through, and scars from those experiences may vary. Black people have diverse political views. Their values may be different based on their religious views. And their commitments to the work of racial justice will likely vary. This means this book is for *white leaders as well as leaders of color*. Tatum (2001) declared,

> In a race-conscious society, the development of a positive sense of racial/ethnic identity not based on assumed superiority or inferiority is an important task for *both* [italics added] White people and people of color. The development of this positive identity is a lifelong process that often requires unlearning the misinformation and stereotypes we have internalized not only about others, but also about ourselves. (p. 53)

Overall, the book is written for every school leader who wants to do what is right. They may not understand racism. These educators may be politically conservative. They may be independent. They may or may not be politically liberal. I have written this book for educators who are diverse in terms of political affiliations, racial and ethnic identities, religious backgrounds, language orientation, and who desire to know what is necessary in the work of anti-racist leadership now, in this era of complex attempts to ruin any efforts to ensure that all young people across the United States have a fighting chance at attending schools that honor their very humanity. These educators may or may not have experienced racism, sexism, homophobia, xenophobia, or other forms of discrimination themselves. But these school leaders are committed to their students, schools, and communities. These school leaders see their responsibility to create spaces where young people think, question, critique, learn, develop, experience joy, and transform. School leaders in the fight for racial justice create contexts where young people are encouraged, supported, and expected to debate and engage with each other in civil, rigorous, caring, empathetic, and humanizing ways. This book is constructed for leaders who are committed to places where young people come to know more deeply themselves, their places in the world, and how they can build tools and skillsets that do more than contribute to their own individual success. This book is for school leaders who want their students to be well-prepared for their everyday lives at schools, well-energized to engage with their families and communities, powerfully prepared for college, and skillfully prepared for career and work. They want them to be well-rounded and prepared to live locally and globally with people who have varying values, belief systems, experiences, and walks of life. But perhaps most importantly, this book is written for school leaders who want their students to experience the fullness of life—to find joy (Muhammad, 2023) now in districts, schools, and classrooms because they understand that their commitments to racial justice are deeply tied to their success and contributions to the world.

I have never known educators to be more afraid to do what they know to be right for young people regarding the design, promotion, and enactment of learning opportunities that are racially just. And, so, I have written this book for the hundreds of school leaders with whom I have worked over the years who are directly experiencing backlash from bullies hoping to derail racial justice agendas of consequence. Consequential agendas are those that can have a real bearing on the lives of young people. I have also written this book to help those in educational leadership programs, those preparing to become school leaders. The book is also for those already in leadership roles, and those preparing to become school leaders must continue building their knowledge, understandings, skills, and practices considering current contexts in which we are living. I have deliberately written this book for leaders drawing from my robust insights about teachers and young people in districts, schools, and classrooms.

About the Author

The Race Card: Leading the Fight for Truth in America's Schools is a book I have developed from many lessons I have learned from teachers, young people, parents, community members, policy advocates, and school leaders over the past 25 years. What I share in *The Race Card* are lessons I have learned as a former high school English teacher, a substitute teacher, a community college instructor who taught in developmental studies, and an educational researcher who has spent hundreds of hours observing classrooms and schools as well as interviewing teachers, students, caregivers, policymakers, and leaders about their practices related to education and equity. Thus, I develop the recommendations, insights, and implications that I share with leaders in this book based on lessons from those in real schools attempting to engage in transformative racial justice work.

Most of my career has been spent studying the lives and practices of teachers in schools, particularly those in middle and high schools. When my twin daughters were born, twelve years ago, my interest expanded to elementary school classrooms as I attempted to learn as much as I could to support my daughters and their educational experience. Thus, I have attempted to write this book to help educational leaders across the grade span—from prekindergarten through grade 12. Moreover, I have spent much time learning with educators and young people in urban schools. In fact, most of my research has been conducted in urban schools.

More recently, I have studied what I call micro-level policies that shape students' opportunities to learn in suburban, independent schools with more material resources. My earliest research, in fact, was conducted in a suburban community and school in Ohio. I then shifted my work to mostly urban schools. I have become extremely concerned about what is (and is not) happening in rural America. When we think about the lack of focus on race in schools and particularly in rural communities, I am increasingly worried that the United States is headed for (if we are not already in) a race war across multiple contexts. Thus, this book is for preK–12 educators across contexts—urban, suburban, and rural.

School Leadership for Racial Justice in Space and Place

The contexts of school leadership for racial justice can be described as urban, suburban, and rural. I often think about the social contexts of our work as knowledge and understanding of the nouns of our space:

the people (diverse, or similar), places (geography of opportunity, e.g., green space, worship centers), things (resources), and ideas (politics, values, visions, and missions) of the community. Schools typically have some connections to the people who live and attend school in the social context, the characteristics of those people, as well as surrounding community realities where the school is situated. Although not well conceptualized, urban and rural communities have many assets and strengths. There is a rich array of excellence, intellect, and talent among the people in urban and rural environments—human capital that make meaningful contributions to the very fabric of the human condition in the United States and abroad. School leadership for racial justice must take place in urban and rural communities, regardless of how those contexts are defined and conceptualized. I introduced several types of urban communities to help describe the places in which our work occurs in schools: urban intensive, urban emergent, and urban characteristic.

Urban intensive communities are contexts that are concentrated in large, metropolitan cities across the United States, such as Houston, New York, Chicago, Los Angeles, and Atlanta. What sets these cities apart from other cities is their size and density. These environments would be considered intensive because of the sheer numbers of people in the city and consequently the schools. In these cities, the infrastructure and large numbers of people can make it difficult to provide necessary and adequate resources to the large numbers of people who need them. In sum, urban intensive speaks to the size and density of a particular locale; the broader environments, outside of school factors such as housing, poverty, greenspace, and transportation, are directly connected to access, opportunity, and what happens inside of a school. Urban intensive environments would be those with one million people or more in the city.

Urban emergent areas are contexts that are typically located in large cities but not as large as the major cities identified in the urban intensive category. These cities typically have fewer than one million people in them but are relatively large contexts, nonetheless. Although they do not experience the magnitude of the challenges that the urban intensive cities face, they do encounter some of the same scarcity of resource problems, but on a smaller scale. In these areas, there are fewer people per capita; the realities of the surrounding communities are not as complex as those in the intensive category, but these cities tend to be experiencing increases in population as people migrate from urban intensive environments.

Urban characteristic environments are often located in traditionally classified rural contexts. These places are not located in big or midsized cities but may be starting to experience some of the challenges and assets associated with urban environments. For instance, in rural communities, there may be an increase in the number of English language learners in the community. Urban characteristic may be those communities that are in rural or even suburban districts, but the outside-of-school environments are not as large as those in the urban intensive or urban emergent schools.

Mostly White Places and Spaces

Frontline Leadership must happen in white spaces just as the work is done in and with communities of color. Ross (2013) described white space as social contexts "where White individuals, whether culturally or physically, are overrepresented" (p. 143), and the overall ethos of the environment is inundated with whiteness to maintain inequitable power structures. Far too many believe that when they are working in communities with mostly white students that race, racism, whiteness, anti-Black racism, and racial justice are tangential to what *really* matters. When there are very few students (and adults) of color in a social context, race is often perceived as absent. Indeed, some educators do not believe race matters in mostly white spaces until they actually experience and/or are forced to confront unsettling situations, such as these:

- Someone in the community makes a racist comment.

- Parents become uncomfortable with inter/cross-racial dating among students.

- Adults in a school start to question why all the members of one racial group sit together during free time, such as at lunch, at an assembly, or during sporting events.

- Parents insist that their students not be taught by a teacher of color.

- Children of color are not invited to outside-of-school gatherings, such as parties and sleepovers, of their white friends.

- It becomes evident that students of color are showcased in sports, while white students are showcased in honors courses, in honor clubs and societies, and/or with academic awards.

- The number of teachers of color is disproportionately low in comparison to the number of white teachers.

- Students and parents become concerned that the school curriculum is drastically Eurocentric.

Frontline Leadership considers the ways in which families, parents, community members, educators, and young people in predominantly white schools and communities experience race, reproduce and reinforce racism, and enact whiteness through violence and harm in their local communities and beyond. While the argument or position about the necessity for understanding and centralizing race typically focuses on what happens when people and students in particular leave mostly white spaces and interact with more racially diverse communities, leaders must understand that the work of race is essential in curriculum, instruction, assessment, and relationships in their mostly white environments as well. White people are raced people. They operate from and benefit from deeply ingrained privileges.

In my research in mostly white spaces, I have learned that (a) Black teachers are expected to be the expert on everything Black; (b) Black teachers are expected to engage in invisible work without recognition or compensation; and (c) Black teachers are expected to agree with the white majority and be "team players," even when they disagree. Black students in white spaces reported that they experienced hurt, anxiety, and disappointment because of not being invited to sleepovers or outside-of-school functions of white students they once believed to be friends. These Black students reported that they had firm and meaningful friendships with white students in the younger grades (kindergarten through middle school), but as the students got older, white students who used to be their friends and who would invite them to outside-of-school functions began to reject them and replace them with other white classmates. Moreover, Black girl students reported how disheartening it was to not be invited to prom in the mostly white space by Black or other raced boys. They shared that the Black boys tended to invite their white classmates instead.

In short, that young people in mostly white spaces do not experience learning opportunities that expect them to interrogate, make sense of, and build knowledge about racial justice is deeply problematic and must be addressed in deliberate ways. Rather than placing the onus of disrupting racism, whiteness, and anti-Black racism on Black and other minoritized communities, white communities must understand and build tools to do the work necessary as we see increasing threats of violence and harm against Black and other communities of color. The time has passed when mostly white schools go about their work without explicit attention to addressing racism, whiteness, and anti-Black racism. White spaces have been described as "dangerous" and "traumatic" (Ross, 2013, p. 143) when people in these spaces are not deliberately working to counter or disrupt oppressive and repressive policies and practices. In short, either educators are working against oppression, or they are working to maintain it.

The Chapters Ahead

In subsequent chapters of this book, I discuss and expand on the eight tenets, features, and principles of Frontline Leadership that I introduced earlier in this chapter. The chapters that follow expand on the following focal areas with the foundational tenets advanced:

- Frontline leaders work to close opportunity gaps and disrupt racism, whiteness, and anti-Black racism (Chapter 2). I focus on *how to* close gaps of opportunity.

- Frontline leaders co-develop systematic plans and designs to combat and confront racial injustice in schools (Chapter 3). I focus on *how to* plan and design for racial justice and equity in schools.

- Frontline leaders stop punishment and pushout practices and amplify curriculum, instructional, assessment, and relational health of schools (Chapter 4). I focus on *how* to build racially just curriculum, instructional, assessment, and relational practices.

- Frontline Leadership moves beyond stale, dated, predetermined, irrelevant, under-responsive, disconnected, and "racially neutral" decision making with an explicit focus on building policy and practices that move us closer to racial justice and equity (Chapter 5). I conclude the book with profiles of problematic practices, provide concluding tools for school transformation, and offer recommendations to support the work of Frontline Leadership moving forward.

More than a book to outline programs we face, the subsequent chapters have been written with concretized ways to move the work of racial justice and equity forward.

Critiques, insights, research findings, and implications discussed throughout this book require readers to use their professional judgment in adopting, transferring, and advancing these recommendations considering the social context. The work of Frontline Leadership for racial justice and equity requires a deep, robust, and rich knowledge and understanding of the social contexts. Because this racial justice work has the potential to improve the very lives and experiences of minoritized communities, readers must approach this work with diligence, care, and context-robust insights about the people, structures, program, projects, and initiatives necessary for racial justice. The truth about the ugly roots and under(Lie)ing causes of racial inequity can be the conduit for powerful transformation to occur. Increasingly, families, parents, community members, policymakers, high school and college students, and educators share with me their discouragement, puzzlement, uneasiness, frustration, and fear about aggressive efforts meant to distort, upend, and disrupt equity. *The Race Card* is a book for all those who dare to dream of a racially just world where young people in schools experience the fullness of their being, capacity, opportunity, and potential.

Conclusions

Frontline Leadership is not easy. Many educators find themselves at a crossroads. What do school leaders do when their local school boards forbid teachers in their school to teach the truth? How do school leaders negotiate and navigate pressures designed to surveil them and question their professional judgment? What do school leaders do when parents and families expect and push them to reify stereotypes and to focus only on narrow, uncritical curriculum? What do school leaders do as high-quality, equity-centered educators are walking away from the profession every single day? On a broader scale, how could any American argue against core values designed to engage in practices of racial justice that improve the human condition and the United States' national identity? Answers to these questions are not arbitrary, happenstance, or rhetorical. These and similar, relevant questions are those that I hope readers will ponder throughout this book.

> How could any American argue against core values designed to engage in practices of racial justice that improve the human condition and the United States' national identity?

How to Close Opportunity Gaps

2

In the previous chapter, I discussed in great depth what Frontline Leadership is, why it is important, and its role in disrupting racism, whiteness, and anti-Black leadership. Closing opportunity gaps necessitates that educators understand what Frontline Leadership is *not*. Frontline Leadership is not about leaders (1) who believe they are all-knowing; (2) who are arrogant, self-centered, and believe they are superior to others; (3) who dictate and tell others what to do without engaging in the work themselves; (4) who ostracize and push young people, families, communities, and colleagues to the margins when they struggle or fail; (5) who embarrass and dehumanize others; (6) who believe their formal education is more significant than the lived experiences of others; (7) who focus on test scores more than the learning and development of educator colleagues, families, and students; (8) who hire and associate only with like-minded friends, confidants, and "yes" people; (9) who hold grudges against the people they are serving and working with; or (10) who view their role and work as transactional. Rather, Frontline Leadership is a way of thinking and is embraced by leaders who understand their responsibility, commitment, and necessity to work with others through deep, profound relationships in co-constructing a healthy, psychologically safe community. Closing opportunity gaps through Frontline Leadership requires special attention to how opportunity gaps are reinforced across different units of practice. In this chapter, I focus on closing opportunity gaps as a foundational principle to advancing tenets of Frontline Leadership.

Opportunity structures are at play on a *micro level* or school level that requires school leaders' attention in the fight to do racial justice work. Building from more than twenty years of research in schools and working with teachers, I have found that educators' mindsets, which shape their practices in education, can have a profound impact on what I have called *opportunity gaps.* I intentionally refer to gaps in education as opportunity gaps rather than achievement gaps because achievement gap conceptualizing and talk place most, if not all, of the blame and responsibility on students and families—those outside of school communities—in our quest to collectively improve educational outcomes and outputs.

Opportunity Gaps Through Color and Race Avoidance

Opportunity gaps escalate when educators adopt a color-blind mindset to their work where they do not acknowledge, honor, and build on students' racial identity in, from, with, and through their curriculum, instructional, assessment, and relational practices. Frontline Leadership understands and acknowledges how individual educators' color-blindness and race-blindness fueled by their beliefs, views, mindsets, paradigms, preferences, and ideologies contribute to systemic, systematic, and institutional patterns such as (a) an over-referral of Black students to the office from classrooms, (b) a disproportionate number of Black students who are suspended and expelled, (c) an overwhelming and disproportionate number of Black students who are referred to special education, and (d) an under-referral of Black and other racialized minoritized students to gifted and advanced placement. These systemic patterns prevalent in schools are concrete examples of practices that lead to gaps in opportunity. Through the study of their school community, frontline leaders recognize, name, nuance, problematize, and work to address these and other emergent challenges that can have a real bearing on student experiences and outcomes.

Opportunity Gaps Through Cultural Conflicts

Opportunity gaps manifest through cultural conflicts between educators and students, schools and communities, and educators and policymakers. These gaps increase when educators do not understand how their own culture and cultural practices are not aligned and are incongruent with their students, families, and communities, resulting in cultural conflicts. It is important to note that I am differentiating between culture and cultural practices here. First, although race influences our culture, race and culture are not the same. Second, culture is dynamic, evolving, and wide ranging. Cultural practices are linked to what we do more than to predetermined conceptions of what we look like, our accents, where we live, or who we are related to. For instance, an educator who speaks Spanish may not be Mexican, Colombian, Venezuelan, Argentinian, or Cuban. That educator's capacity to speak

Spanish is a cultural practice, not necessarily his/her/their culture or ethnicity. Ethnicity is tied to people's ancestral home countries. Frontline Leadership requires that a school environment is designed to embrace and maintain different, diverse, and varied ways of practicing language in a community.

Opportunity Gaps Through the Myth of Meritocracy

Some educators also believe they have earned their "rightful" privileges and affordances because they have worked hard and followed the law or because they have skill, innate capacity, will, and ability. However, they may not understand that conceptions of meritocracy contribute to the expansion of opportunity gaps. Meritocracy does not consider structural inequities that privilege some groups at the expense of others. Rather, it assumes that everyone is on an equal playing field and individual effort alone will (and should!) be rewarded. It also is grounded in an individualistic belief system that is antithetical to collectivism. Frontline Leadership requires that spaces are co-created where people understand that we succeed not solely because of our individual work and practices but because we work and live in community with others. Thus, when leaders focus on and advance meritocracy and do not co-construct a collective community where young people and educators realize our interdependence, the community is established as a place where individual success is seen as the optimal goal and competition is rewarded. Success emerges due to factors beyond merit.

Opportunity Gaps Through Deficit Thinking and Low Expectations

Opportunity gaps also intensify when educators have deficit mindsets and low expectation mindsets of students and communities. These deficit mindsets suggest that students and their families are lacking. Educators may think, believe, and even say that "students have so little," "they lack so much," and "their families do not possess X, Y, Z," rather than focusing on what they DO have (i.e., their assets). Such mindsets show up from conversations educators have with colleagues about students and families, their reading of students' school records, and/or their generalized, misinformed stereotypes of students. Frontline Leadership is focused on co-constructing an ethos where individual and community are viewed as necessary assets in the fabric of success in a school.

> Frontline Leadership is focused on co-constructing an ethos where individual and community are viewed as necessary assets in the fabric of success in a school.

These leaders model their value, respect, and honor of all their students and pay special attention to the ways in which people and communities of color are perceived, responded to, and respected. Such leadership reorients deficit mindsets and low expectations through how they talk about their students: "Our students are brilliant," "Our young people want to succeed," "Our families go above and beyond to support their children and families even in the midst of challenging, racist conditions."

Frontline Leadership redresses, disrupts, and transforms deficit mindsets with meaningful, proactive, and humanizing expectations. These reimagined expectations are raised and responsive to the community. In this way, high expectations are not equated with white, normative expectations. High expectations are equated with excellence that breeds outcomes for young people who have historically been disenfranchised due to racist, implicit and explicit systems designed for them to fail. Rather than watering down learning opportunities (focused on low levels of knowledge and engagement), Frontline Leadership insists that students are challenged and engaged in opportunities to critique what they are learning while building knowledge and skills of transformation.

Opportunity Gaps Through Context Neutrality

Educators do not work in a vacuum but are part of an ecosystem that includes the broader community. Race, racism, anti-Black racism, and whiteness must be understood in the context of encounters. When educators adopt context-neutral mindsets, they have a difficult time understanding the need to study the spaces, places, and overall environments of students and their families. The number of opportunity gaps increase when school leaders and others act as they know best on every front and do not rely on, value, validate, and incorporate the enormous range of expertise, insights, and brilliance in local and broader contexts of their work.

Frontline Leadership and leaders see the community as a vital part of what happens inside of school. Leaders develop mechanisms to learn with, support, and improve their own leadership practices, pedagogical excellence, curriculum rigor and clarity, healthy and sustainable relationships, and rich, deep assessment practices in schools. As educators live and educate themselves outside of the community in which they teach, context neutrality can be a detriment to their decision-making capacity and fortitude. In this way, Frontline Leadership is about moving outside of the walls of a classroom in urban, suburban, and rural social contexts—those that are urban intensive, urban emergent, and urban characteristic. Understanding the confluence of the macro, meso, and micro levels of opportunity gaps necessitates school leaders' awareness of the locus of control regarding these matters. While understanding these issues are essential, the degree to which school leaders can facilitate powerful and impactful changes is much more tenuous.

Opportunity Gaps Through Structures and Systems

Focusing on *opportunity structures and systems* allows us to study, understand, and build knowledge about (to inform practice of) how varying levels of the educational enterprise propel or stifle student learning, development, experiences, and outcomes. Analyzing opportunity structures and systems would insist that we focus on inputs (the experiences) rather than focusing on outputs (outcome variables such as test scores). Opportunity structures are those we might consider on a *macro level* such as how national or even international trends impact our work in schools—*how we think, what we do and do not do, when, on behalf of whom, and why.* For instance, national structures such as immigration policies, firearm laws, and health care policies have a direct impact on access and opportunities educators, families, communities, and young people have in schools. In short, addressing and ending opportunity gaps requires that school leaders understand world and national issues—just as they are laser focused on their immediate school community.

Opportunity structures are also at a *meso level,* or middle level, such as systems that manifest through expectations, musings, policies, and practices in a more localized way but outside of a particular school or district. Meso-level structures are those that may influence schools such as state and community needs and trends, funding and philanthropic supports, and pushback against and support for what school leaders and other educators do in schools and classrooms. An example of macro- and meso-level structures that directly impact what educators do in schools is the backlash and deliberate policies and discourses against teaching Critical Race Theory in preK–12 schools. Although the vastly white teaching force is not teaching Critical Race Theory in schools, these opportunity structures designed to dissuade truth, distort public perception, and maintain racial subordination impact how principals interact with, plan, support, and advance a community of teaching and learning in schools.

Closing Opportunity Gaps Through Language Shifts

Haberman (2000) maintained that "language is not an innocent reflection of how we think. The terms we use control our perceptions, shape our understanding, and lead us to particular proposals for improvement" (p. 203).

Our conceptions, belief systems, knowledge, thinking, ideas, ideologies, frames of reference, cultural practices, and lived experiences shape our discourse patterns. What we believe, think, and believe we know is exhibited in our oral communication with others through our privileges, advantages, and experiences of oppression. Frontline Leadership and leaders are resolute in building a language community of restoration, hope, possibility, and, most importantly, opportunity.

As an educational researcher, I have found that a true sign of the culture of a school is shaped and guided by how people speak about and to others in their community. Ladson-Billings (2006) challenged us to rethink the use of the term *achievement gap* when discussing and explaining test scores and differences between and among groups of students. Ladson-Billings (2006) concluded that in the United States, there is not as much of an achievement gap as there is an "education debt" that the educational system owes to the many students it has poorly served. This education debt carries several important features, according to Ladson-Billings, including a historical debt, economic debt, sociopolitical debt, and moral debt. For instance, centering race and racism, *what* and *how* should the school community understand historical roots of the United States (macro)? *What* and *how* should the school community understand historical assets and challenges of the broader community (meso)? And *what* and *how* should the school community understand historical legacies of the school (micro)? Employing these four frames (historical, economic, sociopolitical, and moral) as research and analytic sites, Ladson-Billings challenged us to reconceptualize and move beyond achievement discourse to address myriad layers of debt owed to so many students in education. Frontline Leadership provides a space for school leaders to facilitate conversations about how the school community will talk and aspire to talk in the work of race. That is, how will the language of the school amplify excellence, assets, and opportunities of racialized students, communities, and educators?

Irvine (2010) outlined several other gaps that must be addressed: "the teacher quality gap; the teacher training gap; the challenging curriculum gap; the school funding gap; the digital divide gap; the wealth and income gap; the employment opportunity gap; the affordable housing gap; the health care gap; the nutrition gap; the school integration gap; and the quality childcare gap" (p. xii). From Irvine's perspective, when we address the many other gaps that structurally and systemically exist in educational practice, achievement results can improve. The opportunity here is to build a school community that interrogates the range of gaps Irvine describes, such as the challenging curriculum gap (micro) to affordable housing (macro) and deciding how language will be used in their own community.

The language of opportunity considers how we talk about and to young people, their families, and communities, as well as each other as educators. Some schools refer to their students as scholars. Others call their students by their last name with a title—Miss Jones, Mr. Roberts. For sure, our language must be inclusive, and Frontline Leadership insists that pronouns and titles are relevant, responsive, and humanizing. However, *while I have observed educators in schools referring to their students as scholars or by their last names, their behavior falls short of their language.* For instance, co-deciding on racially, just, humanizing language is not shallow and correlates with impact and actions. Simply calling students "scholars" or some other type of restorative, supportive label and concurrently treating them like prisoners or members of the military sends deep messages of hypocrisy that young people surely "read," experience, and carry forward.

Language, Self-Worth, and Belonging

As a child, I experienced moments of sustained bullying. When I had problems with classmates, and the disagreements resulted in name-calling or callous language, my parents were quick to refer to an old and well-known adage: "Talk is cheap." Not only was their dismissal of the words that sometimes cut deeply, annoying, but I was frustrated because more times than not "the talk" was not cheap at all. Word, discourse patterns, and language construction can be socially and emotionally damaging, viscious, abusive, and dangerous in schools and classrooms. This means that Frontline Leadership co-cultivates spaces where the language of the school builds up, restores, and supports faculty, staff, young people, families, parents, and community members. In this sense, talk is not cheap, innocent, unharmful, neutral, or inconsequential. In the case of young people experiencing racism, degrading and dehumanizing language and feedback, talk is expensive because that talk typically infiltrates their thoughts and beliefs about themselves.

> Simply calling students "scholars" or some other type of restorative, supportive label and concurrently treating them like prisoners or members of the military sends deep messages of hypocrisy that young people surely "read," experience, and carry forward.

What is important for adults to remember is that many students, and especially adolescents, are grappling with their self-esteem (their *feelings* about themselves, their sense of worth and belonging) and self-efficacy (their *thoughts* and *beliefs* about themselves, their capacity and potential). Young people are often trying to "fit in" and sometimes feel worthless, even when adults believe that the students have everything they need—perhaps in terms of resources and capital—to succeed. But students are often struggling with whether they belong in a school, in a classroom, or among a group of friends or classmates. Language and what young people hear send a message to them about who they are, who they can and should be, whether they belong and/or fit into a community, and the kind of effort they should exude in a community.

However, belonging for people of color and other minoritized students does not mean that they assimilate, adapt, merge, and dissolve into a white normative, oppressive ethos. Banks (1998) stressed that "some groups of students—because their cultural characteristics are more consistent with the culture, norms, and expectations of the school [and their teachers and leaders] than are those of other groups of students—have greater opportunities for academic success than do students whose cultures are less consistent with the school [and teachers' and leaders'] culture" (Banks, 1998, pp. 22–23). Thus, belonging means that, through language and communication, young people construct, claim, and own the contexts in which they are and bring the entirety of their racial identity and other identity markers into space and place.

> Language and what young people hear send a message to them about who they are, who they can and should be, whether they belong and/or fit into a community, and the kind of effort they should exude in a community.

Students, through their socialization, are often implicitly comparing themselves to others, yearning for acceptance from their friends, rivalries, older siblings, teachers, and parents (and sometimes in this order!). Students want to feel accepted; they want to be the boss and authors of their contexts and experiences. Frontline Leadership requires that the language of school builds communities of belonging. The language used to describe a student or even language that is used as a joke can be seriously hurtful to students. It is not enough to practice empathy, where adults put themselves in students' shoes. Our different life experiences sometimes prevent us from being able to deeply empathize with, relate to, care about, advocate for, and talk with others in ways that affirm, restore, heal, build, and sustain students' identity, beliefs, and actions.

When people have not experienced sexism, it may be difficult for them to empathize with another when that person experiences it. Or when people experience one form of discrimination, hate, or another type of *-ism*, they may prioritize solutions that align with their own challenges. Indeed, students' experiences in schools may be qualitatively different than what and how adults experience the same *-ism* in a school. How do educators' comments build up or tear down the spirit of the student? Love (2019) has addressed what she calls "spirit murdering" in her important book, *We Want to Do More Than Survive.*

Language, Intent, and Impact

Intentionality and impact are at the core of language, talk, word choice, and overall discourse patterns in a school. While educators' intentions may be genuine or even encouraging, the impact can be damaging. For instance, what may be considered "just joking around" to one person may be interpreted as completely inappropriate to another person. Consider the following exchanges and the ways in which intentionality could be conflated with impact:

- To a Black student: Have a seat, boy.

- To a self-identified male student: You hit like a girl.

- To a student from a lower socioeconomic background: You need to purchase a new pair of khakis that fit.

- To a student new to the school: That may be how you did things "over there" but not here.

- To a Korean American student: We are so glad to have you in *our* school. You bring diversity to *us*.

- To an American Indian student: No, but where are you really from?

- To a white student: You don't know what it's like to experience discrimination.

- To a Jewish student: Can we get over the Holocaust?

What is absent from these comments is contextual grounding. There is no information about the identity of the speaker or the nature of the relationships between and among the speaker and hearer. Frontline Leadership cultivates spaces where these questions are constantly being considered to address potential impact. Sadly, what happens in many communities that claim to have good intentions is that silence is the language of communication when disagreement is present or when talk deals with a sensitive issue, such as racist, homophobic, or sexist (or their intersected) comments, for instance. Delpit (1995) writes extensively about the notion of silence as a form of communication and what she called the "silent dialogue" in her important book, *Other People's Children: Cultural Conflict in the Classroom.* Educators are communicating something even when they are silent.

Frontline Leadership is essential to the language of school because the ways in which people interpret silence can vary. For example, when educators witness racist, insensitive comments and say nothing, formally or informally, they are in essence communicating and teaching their students something. Also, the people who make the insensitive comments are communicated with even though the silent voices can have multiple meanings and intentions. Those who communicate the racist and insensitive language may believe that silence is a sign of acceptability; they may believe, based on silence, that their language is tolerable because no one has spoken out against it. Again, neutrality and silence are forms of acceptance. Either educators are working toward anti-racist, anti-oppressive, and opportunity-centered language, or they are working against it. Critical theorist Freire (1998) explained that it is the responsibility of those who have power to use it when they witness and/or experience injustice. Frontline Leadership demands that young people are encouraged (taught if they are not accustomed to encouragement) and expected to speak up and speak out against racist, dehumanizing, oppressive language. In short, talk is behavior, and educators must be challenged and have the conviction to act when they witness language injustice. The idea of *speaking up and speaking out* is especially important when the victim—the vulnerable, the person on the receiving end of the hurtful language—cannot speak out due to power structures that prevent them. To recap, Frontline Leadership communicates that silent voices are voices that are speaking!

> Silent voices are voices that are speaking!

Language as Action and Reinforcement of Hurt and Harm

Language is action; it is not some innocent consequence of people's intentionality. What I have learned is that hurting people are more likely to hurt people; that is, those who have experienced and are working through trauma, pain, violence, and stress are more likely to inflict practices on others through their words (even unintentionally). However, the point here is not that all hurting people hurt others. The point is that when hurting people are not consciously working toward restoration, healing, and improvement, they are more likely to cause harm to others through their discourse. Thus, Frontline Leadership co-creates an environment of wellness and spaces where people can pursue healing themselves—just as they co-develop spaces of healing for the young people with whom they work. School leaders understand that educators will have different views on the role, salience, and potential impact of race and racism in society and schools. This means that focusing on and centralizing race and racism to disrupt and dismantle them will require their engagement with a range of -*isms* that open space for race. Addressing the self and community, frontline leaders consider advancing the following questions: What are you prepared to do when you hear or experience racist, sexist, homophobic, or xenophobic (i.e., inappropriate and insensitive) language? What are we prepared to do as a community when we hear and/or experience racist, sexist, homophobic, or xenophobic (inappropriate and insensitive) language?

Martin Luther King Jr. shared a point that is extremely relevant for these times: "In the end, we will remember not the words of our enemies, but the silence of our friends." While we are encouraged by those who are vocal in this moment as we fight for racial justice, we are concurrently struck by the scores of people from different racial and socioeconomic backgrounds who remain silent. Liberals, conservatives, and those in between can be guilty of disengagement, avoidance, and overall muteness in districts, schools, and classrooms. They go about their daily affairs as if nothing is happening, not talking to students about how they are doing, not holding their colleagues and sometimes other students accountable when they invoke deficit, racist, demeaning, and anti-Black racist language. Moreover, some educators refuse to utter the words "Black Lives Matter." Although they would claim to believe Black lives matter, their arrogance, privileges, and disdain for Blackness will not allow them to speak the words.

For too many, those who remain silent claim that they actually do care about and empathize with communities of color. However, in the powerful words of James Baldwin, "I can't believe what you say because I see what you do." Troubling, there are several reasons people decide not to speak out for racial justice and against racism, whiteness, and anti-Black racism.

- Some people believe their silence in the face of injustice somehow will save them from the ugliness of racism and discrimination writ large. They rationalize that things will just work out and that they should have no role in speaking out against injustice or doing anything otherwise.

- Some people believe their educational level and professional and social status will save them. In this sense, people concentrate on and believe the fallacy that their perceived status and stature somehow make them "better" or "above" others. Thus, they opt not to speak out.

- Some people do not believe or realize how detrimental to the psychological, emotional, and mental health racist, regressive, and harmful language can be for positive outcomes, practices, and outputs.

Sometimes Students Just Need a Communicated "Win"

Frontline Leadership sees language of opportunity as a socially constructed imperative that those in the community create, advance, and cultivate. For instance, we socially construct achievement and success. Certain areas of achievement are privileged and valued over others, and there appears to be a socially constructed hierarchy of *which* and *what* achievements, success, and knowledge matter more than others in schools. The way we as adults communicate our perceptions of success and achievement in schools sends important messages to students. In short, I have found that some young people just need a communicated win.

These students, many of whom are those of color, are traversing spaces not designed for them. They put all their efforts in and almost never receive opportunity-rich feedback and encouragement. These students do not (and likely will never) make the honor roll. These students are not (and likely will never be) the star athletes in school. These students do not (and likely will never) have the lead or even a major supporting role in the school play. And, thus, these students feel excluded, not good enough, and like "losers" in the broad community of the school. But our language can be a difference maker in the lives of these young people.

> Our language can be a difference maker in the lives of these young people.

Unfortunately, the knowledge, success, and skills of students of color are often seen as substandard or not as essential in the big picture of what is really valued. Our discourse patterns create societal and school-related high and low cultural ways of identifying and honoring skills, knowledge, achievement, and success (Duncan-Andrade & Morrell, 2005). For instance, in literacy instruction, white ways of knowing and knowledge about and achievement related to traditional canonical readings from authors such as William Shakespeare or Charles Dickens are considered high culture, whereas African (American) literature written by authors such as Zora Neale Hurston or James Baldwin may be classified as low culture. These links between language, conceptions of what knowledge matters and should be taught, the value of what is covered, and how we talk to and about students are deeply connected and should be addressed in school communities. Frontline leaders may facilitate questions (such as those below) as they co-construct language of opportunity. Frontline leaders realize that our language is necessarily aligned with our mindsets, beliefs, knowing, thinking, and worldviews about *what matters, who matters, when they matter, why they matter,* and *what we do* to create humanizing places that press against racism, whiteness, and anti-Black racism. A convergence of language of opportunity and how schools co-construct and talk about success can be queried through reflective questions such as the following:

- To what extent is achievement synonymous with and divergent from learning?

- What do we value as successful, and who do we identify as knowledgeable in our school?

- Who constructs knowledge in the school, from what sources, and for what purposes?

- What does it mean for individuals and groups of students to learn and achieve in our schools?

- Who decides what it means to achieve, learn, and succeed in our schools and why?

- How do we know when young people are succeeding, and what are our assessment tools to determine this success?

- How do we honor and acknowledge learning among those who have been grossly underserved in schools and communities?

- How do we address and assess the kind of learning and knowledge acquisition that never shows up on achievement measures, including formative assessments and high-stakes, standardized tests?

Frontline Leadership ensures that the school community reflects on such questions in the press toward racial justice and equity.

Building Frontline Leadership Muscles

Drawing from my own empirical research over the past couple of decades, I have outlined six interrelated imperatives that school leaders must consider as they build their curriculum, instructional, assessment, and relational muscles—a point that I will expand upon in this chapter and throughout this book.

- Frontline Leadership practices centralize and cultivate relationships with young people, colleagues in school, families, parents, community advocates, policymakers, and educational researchers. It is important to note that educational researchers should be resources for school leaders to stay current in research findings necessary to advocate for racial justice and truth during moments when pundits are suppressing learning opportunities to maintain whiteness.

- Frontline Leadership practices build on and from community knowledge to inform practice. Restressing the point that school leaders are not, should not, and cannot be all-knowing, building deliberate practices to learn with community about racial issues is a strategy that will take leaders far in the fight for racial justice. Community knowledge is developed when school leaders live in the community in which they are teaching. I call living this form of community learning to build knowledge, *community immersion*. And if educators cannot live in the community of their students, their racial knowledge can be enhanced through *community engagement*, where educators are actively involved in school boards, community organizations, and so forth. Still another aspect of community learning to enhance educator knowledge is what I call *community attendance*, which may mean that while educators are not actively engaged in community affairs, they show up and participate in solidarity with others in the community. A fourth feature of community learning is what I call *community investment*, which allows educators to extend some of their capital and resources to the community in which they teach. This investment may be as simple as getting a haircut in the community, ordering food from a community vendor, or spending time tutoring at the local recreation center. In all cases, educators learn about and from those in the community—this community knowledge should inform their practices. I summarize these different forms of community knowledge to inform practice in Figure 2.1.

FIGURE 2.1   Community Knowledge to Inform Practice

Building Community
Knowledge
to Address Race

COMMUNITY IMMERSION

Living in your community of students and schools for community learning

COMMUNITY ENGAGEMENT

Engaging, participating, and joining in community affairs such as education councils and board meetings to support schools and classrooms

COMMUNITY ATTENDANCE

Attending student events in the community (plays, sporting events, concerts)

COMMUNITY INVESTMENT

Spending and offering your financial support and other resources within the community to your students and school (time, capital, funds)

- Frontline Leadership practices stress and advance psychological and mental health among students, school personnel, families, and communities of the school. Too often, school leaders do not recognize that psychological strain, mental health challenges, and traumatic experiences can be school induced. To be clear, although unintentional, schools can produce and reify racism that leads to mental, emotional, and psychological stress. According to the World Health Organization (n.d.), "Mental health is a state of well-being in which an individual realizes [his, her, their] own abilities, can cope with normal stresses of life, can work productively, and is able to make a contribution to [his, her, their] community." An important question for school leaders is who decides what "normal stresses" are and what counts as "normal stresses." Especially in the case of racism, whiteness, and anti-Black racism, it can be difficult to determine normality.

- Frontline Leadership practices converge the curriculum. In the fight for racial justice, I am advancing the idea that curriculum convergence[1] can be a game changer in a school. From a racial justice standpoint, curriculum convergence begins with the premise that the "so what" of learning opportunities is just as important as what is being taught. Young people, and Black students especially, spend countless hours in classrooms engaged in learning tasks that are too often disconnected from anything that meaningfully resonates with them, their communities, and their experiences. Curriculum convergence allows for dynamic, iterative, and agile learning opportunities as it recognizes, honors, and builds on students' developing, changing, and varied identities; connects with community realities; and reflects students' evolving interests and motivations by acknowledging their *extra* curriculum engagement (such as art, music, sport, and dance). Curriculum convergence merges the who (student identity), the what (community and society as texts), and the where (outside of school engagement of young people) by shepherding young people into spaces where they apply what they are learning and experiencing to something much greater than what might be expected of them through an assignment or assessment in a school or classroom. Curriculum convergence pushes a discourse that continually asks young people and educators to answer the "so what" of opportunities to learn.

---

[1]Other scholarship has discussed the idea of curriculum convergence (see, e.g., https://www.tandfonline.com/doi/abs/10.1080/03050060120103856?journalCode=cced20; https://www.tandfonline.com/doi/abs/10.1080/03075079.2016.1190704?journalCode=cshe20).

It demands that we reimagine canonical ways of constructing the curriculum across different subject areas (e.g., mathematics, science, social studies, and literacy).

- Frontline Leadership practices push the curriculum to social action. *Social action* and *activism* should be viewed as the highest form of a curriculum as the curriculum is constructed with the intentional and consistent goal of application. Banks's (1998) model of curricula integration and transformation is a powerful tool to think about pushing the curriculum to social action. Banks outlined several levels of curriculum work that frontline leaders must consider on a classroom and entire school level: the contributions approach (low level), the additive approach (low level), the transformative approach (high level), and the social action approach (highest level). The contributions level occurs when the curriculum focuses on disconnected individuals in a school or classroom. Rather than revising an entire curriculum, educators highlight the contributions of exemplary, mainstream, nonthreatening, and noncontroversial individuals and their contributions, such as Sonia Sotomayor, Mahatma Gandhi, or Mae C. Jemison. Another low level of curriculum transformation is what Banks calls the additive level. The additive level tinkers around the edges of curriculum reform similar to the contributions level. The additive level moves beyond an individual contribution to a week or even a month of racially and ethnically diverse communities. Most schools that espouse a racially just environment are currently operationalizing curriculum at this level. They celebrate Black History Month, Women's History Month, and Latinx Month. However, the fabric, essence, and value of the curriculum remains firmly tied to whiteness. The transformational approach is a more ideal level when conceiving curriculum revision. The transformation level insists that educators change their minds about what the curriculum is and how it should be enacted. In other words, this level of curriculum reform shepherds students into building tools to critically examine what they are learning and what is missing from the curriculum. And the highest level of curriculum integration and reformation is the social action approach. That is, school leaders work to design with young people opportunities for them to build tools for something greater than what a school assignment might require to complete a task or assessment. Rather, school leaders encourage classroom and broader school opportunities for young people to do something to improve the human condition— to disrupt racism, whiteness, and anti-Black racism.

- Frontline Leadership practices disrupt deficit beliefs about students. Educators have deep (implicit and explicit) negative

views about far too many students of color and their capacity.
Rooted in misnomers and lies about some minoritized students'
intellect, capacity, work ethics, motivation, and possibilities,
educators conceptualize students of color as deficits, incomplete
young people incapable of success. The work of the school leader
is critical in challenging and moving away from these mindsets
and beliefs to center on the many assets that students possess,
develop, and enact in classrooms and schools. I strongly encourage
school leaders to build community contexts that build students'
confidence—their sense of self-efficacy—to combat the many
negative self-perceptions students of color may have. Self-efficacy
is predicted to be a strong indicator of student success because
it is deeply tied to student beliefs about their capacity. Whereas
self-esteem is related to student feelings about their capacity, self-
efficacy is linked to their deeply ingrained beliefs concerning their
capacity to succeed. Thus, self-efficacy concerns people's beliefs
about their abilities and capacity to be successful in a domain or a
specific task. Bandura (1986, 1996) identified four sources that can
improve or diminish beliefs (and consequently outcomes). These
four sources include the interpretation of the following: (1) mastery
experiences, (2) physiological and emotional experiences, (3) verbal
and social persuasion experiences, and (4) vicarious experiences.
The most potent way for school leaders to change deficit beliefs is
mastery experiences. *Mastery experiences* are those where young
people actually experience success and are able to reflect on those
successes when conceiving of their ability in future tasks. A second
source of self-efficacy, *physiological experiences*, deals with how
young people interpret and handle emotions such as anxiety,
stress, arousal, and fatigue in carrying out tasks. If young people
understand that these physiological states are normal, they have
a better chance at moving away from deficit views of themselves.
Verbal persuasion, a third source identified by Bandura, relates to
the ways educators talk to students about their capacity to succeed.
Of course, this source of efficacy depends heavily on the verbal
persuader. Specifically, verbal persuasion experiences depend on
the trustworthiness, expertise, and credibility of the persuader
(Bandura, 1986). If an educator does not have a meaningful
relationship with the young person, he, she, or they may not be
convinced of the positive verbal persuading: "You can do this."
"I believe in you." "You are a hard worker." "You are smart." The
fourth source of efficacy, vicarious experiences, concerns those
experiences and tasks that are modeled by someone else. In other
words, *vicarious experiences* concern the extent to which a person's
confidence is informed by watching other people perform a similar,

specific task, or even reading about it in articles or textbooks. Of course, self-efficacy is increased when the young person has a meaningful relationship with or can relate to the person he, she, or they are observing and experiencing the task with vicariously. See Table 2.1 for an organizational representation of self-efficacy to disrupt deficit beliefs.

TABLE 2.1   Building Self-Efficacy to Disrupt Deficit Beliefs

SOURCE	DISRUPTIVE AND ASSET PRACTICES
Mastery Experiences	Practices where young people experience success and can reflect on those successes when conceiving of their ability in future tasks. Educators intentionally create spaces so that young people have sustained and sustainable achievements and successes from which to reflect and build their positive beliefs about their own capacity and abilities to succeed.
Physiological Experiences	Practices where young people study, interpret, and can handle emotions such as anxiety, stress, arousal, and fatigue in carrying out tasks. Educators deliberately facilitate practices where young people can understand that their physiological states are not a final negative determinant of their success and that they still can be successful even when they are stressed. Educators help young people name and work through emotional stress.
Verbal Persuasion	Practices of discourse that speak life, possibility, and encouragement to young people about their capacity to succeed. Educators build relationships with students so that they build trust and believe them when they share with young people that young people can indeed succeed during challenging situations academically, emotionally, and socially.
Vicarious Experiences	Practices where young people see the success of other people whom they relate to in executing tasks. Educators provide opportunities for young people to see, witness, read about, and interact with identity relatable people who have succeeded and mastered experiences, expectations, and challenges that young people are approaching.

Source: Bandura (1986).

Closing Opportunity Gaps Through Relational Practices

Teachers, counselors, leaders, administrators, social workers, caregivers, and young people consistently identify the importance of relationships as a core component of teaching and learning in all types of contexts (Gay, 2010; Howard, 2010; Ladson-Billings, 2009; Milner, 2020c). But educators are rarely overtly prepared to forge the kinds of relationships that can potentially serve as bridges in classrooms and schools. Relationships can be conceptualized as a form of curriculum and pedagogy. What I mean is Frontline Leadership views learning opportunities, instructional moves, and overall classroom construction as the object (curriculum) and mechanism (pedagogy) of teaching and learning in relation with others. By curriculum, I mean what students have an opportunity to learn. By instruction, I mean how the curriculum is taught. Frontline Leadership stresses the importance of building a classroom culture and community that propels and cultivates trust, values racial and other dimensions of diversity, and ensures that every person in the space is whole and well and experiences a deep sense of worth and belonging. In relationship-centered curriculum and pedagogy, students and educators co-build a classroom ethos that considers the evolving and conflicting nature of relationships as a real, central curriculum site.

Essential questions that guide a relationship-centered curriculum and pedagogy include:

- How do we build a school and classroom culture that recognizes and honors the humanity of all?

- What issues can unnecessarily divide us, and what unites us in schools and classrooms?

- What assets do each of us bring into the school and classroom?

- As we build our classroom (and school) communities, how do we honor and build on the many strengths in our decision making and practices?

Some may believe that focusing on the essence of relationships as a legitimate curriculum space is tangential to, inconsequential for, or irrelevant to the expected curriculum of schools (curricular expectations that focus on math, English language arts, science, art, or history, for instance). However, focusing on aspects of these subjects without understanding the complexities of students' experiences can leave some students, often students of color, underserved in schools.

In essence, some students find it difficult to learn from teachers who do not have (or at least have not demonstrated) a strong level of concern for them (Milner, 2020c). My point is Frontline Leadership embraces the reality that without relationship cultivation, we will see persistent racial injustices such as alarming punishment practices of students in classrooms, persistent office referrals, missed instructional time for students who are pushed out of classrooms, student suspensions and expulsions, and the building of walls between educators and families.

Frontline Leadership and Disruptive Movement

Elsewhere I conceptualized and wrote about what I call "disruptive movement" in researching and discussing a science of reading (Milner, 2020b, 2020c). I am extending the work on disruptive movement to Frontline Leadership because similar practices are necessary in the work of racial justice in schools. Similar to building and advancing knowledge about reading, Frontline Leadership disrupts (Milner, 2008), counters (Milner & Howard, 2013), nuances, and exposes (Milner, 2020a, 2020b) storylines, policies, and practices that center and maintain racism, whiteness, and anti-Black racism. Drawing from critical theories of race and political science, several features of disruption and movement are essential as school leaders co-interrogate and co-create spaces of healing, wellness, possibility, passion, opportunity, and transformation. Foundationally, Frontline Leadership (a) exposes the inequitable, the unjust, the irrational, the marginalizing, the minoritizing, the racism; (b) disrupts the racist, inequitable, homophobic, xenophobic, and sexist worldviews, policies, and practices that maintain master narratives or storylines that perpetuate whiteness; and (c) co-facilitates movement for individual, community, collective, and structural change. More than simply exposing, Frontline Leadership advances organizing their colleagues, community members, families, parents, and *young people* to do something—to disrupt and transform systems, policies, and practices and replace them with those that at the very core improve the human condition. Frontline Leadership illuminates, names, and helps others understand the ways in which inequity and collective efforts change and transform existing norms to those that are emancipatory and just. Similar to social movements, Frontline Leadership "emerge[s] purposefully" (Cornfield & Fletcher, 1998, p. 1306), and communities organize themselves around an idea in movements to bring about change (Morris, 1984).

Indeed, COVID-19 has required educators to shift their practices drastically to meet the needs of their students, even as educators worked to take care of themselves and their own families. With such unexpected changes emerged some discourse, concerns, mindsets, and practices that I found counterintuitive to humanizing engagements necessary for collective success. As a major tenet of Frontline Leadership, so much of the work of building spaces for racial justice is embedded in the way we think about our work, our role, our students, and the communities in which we work. Thus, Frontline Leadership requires significant paradigm shifts for those of us in education because many of us have been socialized and brainwashed into believing that practices, policies, engagements, and interactions pre-COVID-19 were the ones that we should return to. For communities of color, where the system was not working or at best where communities of color had to change themselves to thrive, returning to normal is less than ideal. Frontline Leadership calls out (uses language) and disrupts and stops (takes action) oppressive, repressive, racist, sexist, anti-Black, and overall discriminatory mindsets and ways of doing, thinking about, and engaging with education. Frontline Leadership pursues and presses toward a more racially just society and schools while recognizing the ways in which white supremacy is powerfully and interconnectedly woven within and throughout the very policies, institutions, and systems of education and society. The degree to which schools are committed to dismantling white supremacy depends in large part on school leaders' will, fortitude, and drive to build systematic, conscientious, and deliberate analyses that *disrupt* racial injustice and work to *move* practices forward that give Black and other racially minoritized students a fighting chance at educational and life success.

Frontline Leadership is not only about action that manifests through critique. Frontline Leadership is committed to short- and long-term solutions (initiatives to start, replace, innovate, and advance racial justice and equity). For instance, Frontline Leadership

1. *Calls out, disrupts, and stops* languaging that suggests minoritized communities are falling behind more privileged students due to missed instructional time as a result of COVID-19. Frontline Leadership co-cultivates spaces where our focus in education is on the health and wellness of bodies, not on some predetermined socially constructed set of outcomes and milestones that leave minoritized communities even more concerned and worried about their children during a pandemic that no one controlled. Frontline Leadership stresses that families on the margins—many times Black and Brown families—feel an increased level of anxiety as educational systems send the message that these young people are going to be even "more inadequate" and "behind" in a downright racist, classist, white-centric educational and societal system. While communities are grieving over the loss of family members, working through financial hardships, and trying to stay healthy themselves, minoritized communities do not want or need to hear disingenuous forecasts about learning loss. Frontline Leadership calls out, disrupts, and stops this focus on discourse. Frontline Leadership insists that, as individuals and communities, they *start* focusing on the health and wellness of students, parents, families, and communities and work with students where they are in order to learn and develop. Frontline Leadership resists a traditional propensity to center achievement and outcomes through lenses of competitions and comparisons between groups of students where

> Frontline Leadership
> co-envisions and
> co-implements
> spaces where rest and
> recharging are core
> aspects of how they
> conceptualize a thriving,
> vibrant, rigorous, and
> healthy environment.

white students (for which the curriculum, pedagogy, assessments, and systems were designed) almost always outperform students and communities of color.

2. *Calls out, disrupts, and stops* expecting educators and young people to "catch up" and otherwise work during their scheduled breaks. Gloria Ladson-Billings has warned us about focusing on "catch-up" orientations to our work. As communities work through all types of situations within and outside of their control, Frontline Leadership co-envisions and co-implements spaces where rest and recharging are core aspects of how they conceptualize a thriving, vibrant, rigorous, and healthy environment. Frontline Leadership understands that communities of color, in particular, are navigating and working through racism coupled with all the other challenges of living and learning, and they need time to rest. When educators assign homework over winter, spring, and other breaks, entire families are affected and in effect are being punished in the disguise of academic learning and development. To the contrary, Frontline Leadership understands that the social, emotional, mental, and physical health of those in the community fuel academic success. People are tired and need time to recharge. Resting, thinking, planning, and recentering are essential activities during outside-of-school time. Frontline Leadership honors educators' planning times by not assigning them to substitute other teachers' classes when they are absent, for instance.

3. *Calls out, disrupts, and stops* holding similar expectations of students as educators held pre-COVID-19. Frontline leaders understand that high expectations of young people are essential and also context specific. High and rigorous expectations are guided by what students need and experience inside and outside of the school community. Frontline Leadership embraces (not mourns) the reality that COVID-19 has made life different, and we must respond by co-creating contexts with expectations that bring joy and possibility in the spaces of education. Context-specific expectations through Frontline Leadership illuminate the data showing how communities of color were disproportionately affected by COVID-19. Proportionately across the nation, more Black families were hospitalized and died than any other racialized group. This means that Frontline Leadership acknowledges and supports the healing and sustainability of these communities while simultaneously insisting that others

> Frontline Leadership
> understands that the
> social, emotional, mental,
> and physical health of
> those in the community
> fuel academic success.

co-construct an ethos of care, empathy, love, and restoration in school and broader communities. Frontline Leadership identifies the best of what is already established and *starts* to build new and innovative policies and practices that respond to our new normal—a world where we have all lived through a possibly once-in-a-lifetime pandemic that adversely affected all of us but was catastrophic for racial minoritized communities.

4. *Calls out, disrupts, and stops* asking educators to spend their work and nonwork time completing nonsensical tasks that they were forced to complete and engage pre-COVID-19. *Start* listening to educators about what they need and should engage in.

5. *Calls out, disrupts, and stops* assigning letter grades to students. Students are far more than any letter grade might demonstrate. *Start* providing substantive, in-depth, formative, and summative qualitative feedback to students and families to communicate student learning and development over, in, and through the short and long term.

6. *Calls out, disrupts, and stops* being miserable because educators must find new ways to do education. *Start* finding and building tools and mechanisms that result in joy among students, families, and communities.

TABLE 2.2   Disruptive Movement for Creating an Ethos of Racial Justice

DISRUPTIVE	MOVEMENT
Stop communicating that young people are failing.	*Start* focusing on the assets of the young people in front of you and building the health and wellness of the school community.
Stop demanding that young people "catch up" to where they would be if the COVID-19 pandemic hadn't occurred.	*Start* honoring the diligence and resilience of the educators, families, and communities who have survived, and press toward a community of thriving.
Stop having the same expectations of young people and educators before the pandemic, and stop yearning for a return to pre-COVID-19 conditions.	*Start* imagining a new way of doing education focused on the physical, psychological, emotional, social, and educational wellness of all.
Stop educators from engaging in mundane, unresponsive, and irrelevant tasks that have no real bearing on student success.	*Start* learning from and working with educators to co-construct an ethos of racial justice and joy.
Stop assigning traditional letter grades to students.	*Start* advocating for a new paradigm of assessments in schools and districts, tools that are humanizing and community centered.
Stop being so miserable, irritable, hopeless, and regressive to racial justice.	*Start* remembering the "why" of your work and the possibilities embedded in the work of educating young people.

Table 2.2 captures the Frontline Leadership practices I advance for disruption and movement toward racial justice and equity. Frontline leaders stress that, as educators, we have an audacious opportunity to transform how we think and what we do in education to co-create the kinds of learning environments where young people deserve to be.

Reimagine Assessment Practices

Frontline Leadership moves away from assigning letter and numeric grades. Since March 2020, when school systems across the United States and world were forced to move to some form of virtual platforms for teaching and learning, students, parents, and families have expressed concerns about students' grades. High school seniors, for instance, worried about how virtual learning might impact their grade point averages as they applied to colleges and universities. While working full-time jobs (some transitioning to work at home, others negotiating work and careers outside of the home), and caring for family members becoming ill from or even dying of the coronavirus, parents, families, communities, and students worried about how they would support their children's educational learning and development at home. Families of children who learn "differently" were very concerned. One parent in Nashville talked about how her daughter with a "disability" was reportedly failing all her classes. A report in Nashville, Tennessee, revealed that nearly one in five public school students was "failing" at least one class (see https://www.newschan nel5.com/rebound/safely-back-to-school/nearly-1-in-5-metro-nash ville-public-schools-students-failing-at-least-one-class).

Nashville is not the only city reporting an alarming number of students receiving grades of F. How can we maintain the same or a similar grading metric during times of unprecedented challenge? As educators and through Frontline Leadership, we have a responsibility to reimagine our predetermined mindsets about how to evaluate students' progress. Part of that rethinking and reimagining must include the elimination of grades as we have known them in the past. In short, I stress that no student should be told he, she, or they are failing. We should be finding alternative ways to support student learning through assessments that tell educators what they need to know to improve their curriculum, instructional, and relational practices with young people.

Why Stop Assigning Grades?

1. Grades are too often used as weapons that harm the psychological, emotional, and affective health of students and families.

2. Letter and numeric grades can be an abusive tool that causes violence against young people whose experiences, cultural practices, and behaviors are inconsistent with those of the educators and the school.

3. Grades perpetuate an unnecessary and relentless ethos of competition between and among students.

4. Grades force educators (especially teachers) to place a number and/or letter value on developing students. Such grades cannot capture the complexity and diverse range of student learning, development, knowledge, understanding, and, consequently, growth.

5. Grades can contribute to students' lack of confidence and self-esteem because they send a message about worth and value. For instance, students may start to see themselves as a "B" student in math or a "D" student in history.

If Not Traditional Grades, Then What?

To be clear, among the 14,000 school districts across the United States, schools and districts have already begun thinking about, talking about, and changing grading policies. These changes include shifts to practices (and conversations) about Pass/Fail to not having grades at all (see, e.g., https://www.nytimes.com/2020/04/06/learning/coronavirus-schools-grading.html and https://www.insidehighered.com/news/2020/11/30/students-seek-pass-fail-options-again-fall-light-covid-19).

However, as educators, we have been preconditioned to assign grades, not necessarily because we believe they best reflect our assessment of student learning and development but because this is the way "we've always done it." However, frontline leaders reimagine and redefine the work we do as educators with students; grades and grading should be innovatively reimagined for educational transformation. In other words, what about the residual effects of the pandemic that will likely linger for decades? Now that students are physically back in schools, they will still be working through deep and broad levels of grief, stress, heartache, and trauma. Traditional numeric grades, particularly for those most vulnerable (such as students of color), will likely only exacerbate these students' (and families') challenges.

Rather than a focus on traditional grades, Frontline leaders might consider the following:

1. *Recentering the goals of assessment practices.* For too many, assessments do little to provide the kind of feedback to students and educators that propels teaching and learning.

2. *Building stronger mechanisms, more responsive tools,* and *more relevant framing* about what grades can (and should) do for us. Formative assessments, which demonstrate students' learning and development over time, can provide ongoing feedback to students that helps them learn and develop incrementally. This type of assessment moves away from traditional end-of-semester, end-of-quarter, or end-of-term grades where some young people are compared to the white student norm—white students for whom the world works and for whom schools have been designed.

3. *Working with educators on portfolio assessments* that provide multilayered qualitative feedback assessments. Teachers need time to provide written feedback to students that goes beyond traditional letter and numeric grades. This means that Frontline Leadership reimagines scheduling with adequate time for educators to narrate student learning and development.

4. *Constructing summative tools* that capture student learning and development. Summative tools should build on formative assessments that tell a more comprehensive story about student learning and development. In this way, educators are not creating narratives about student learning and development at one time (the end of a term). Rather, when assessments are designed to be restorative and racially sensitive—through approaches that de-center whiteness—narrated student success, learning, and areas for growth are incrementally developed over the entire course of study.

5. *Reallocating, rethinking, and rearranging time* throughout the school day and school year for students and families to talk about formative and summative assessments together. Although written assessments of any kind can provide important insights about

teaching and learning, dialoguing about growth and needs can perhaps be even more illuminating. Dialogue elicits a two-way form of assessment where students and families "speak back" to educators about student learning and development. In this way, families have a chance to tell their side of student learning, and families build a level of agency and connectedness to schools that can make a difference in students' experience.

6. *Supporting, listening to, and involving students* in assessing and evaluating their own work. Students benefit from opportunities to talk with their teachers and caregivers about their learning, development, and areas that need to improve. Cultivating students' capacity to evaluate their own work can provide an important dimension in an evaluation cycle. For sure, assessments without the voices of students perpetuate a cycle of exclusion where young people are forced to just accept dehumanizing practices that may perpetuate an unjust status quo.

To be sure, the young people who benefit and succeed the most in our traditional grading systems are white. Just as the educational system is designed for these students, so too are the grading mechanisms that are prevalent and maintained in school districts across the United States.

Although different from what we are accustomed to, Frontline Leadership disrupts traditional grading practices in schools. I recall a time when people said colleges and universities would never cease the use of the GRE for graduate school admissions. Today, because some institutions have decided to shift their emphases, institutions of higher education are rethinking their reliance on the GRE as the main criterion for college admissions. Surely, as we have lived through a pandemic, we have the capacity to place a permanent moratorium on traditional, numeric grading systems as a racial equity imperative.

How to Co-Develop Systematic Plans and Designs

3

//

Frontline Leadership is committed to drafting and revising a vision that explicitly works against racism, whiteness, and anti-Black racism. This means that the language of where the work of school is heading must overtly, unapologetically, be racially inclusive, equity oriented, and justice forward. Frontline leaders study the vision, rework it for all, and ensure those in the community know it and work through the mission to accomplish it. Frontline Leadership uses deliberate planning and designing to actualize the vision through everyday practices. Thus, frontline leaders understand that the vision of a school is where the school is headed, and the mission is what educators do in their practices to reach the vision.

Frontline Leadership cannot be practiced effectively alone. In my own work as a leader, I have come to realize that my leadership practices succeed when we build, support, cultivate, and sustain a justice-centered, Frontline Leadership team—a collective of people whose focused work and mission are dedicated to the health and wellness of a community and school, through policies and practices. No one person has the capacity to understand and advance an organization without a collective of people who see the value of ensuring that every single person in the community experiences and participates in creating a more racially just and humanizing space. Sadly, too many racial justice leadership narratives—and especially leadership practices in Black communities and of Black people—tend to highlight a lone "savior," a person who "whips" their teachers, staff, students, and even parents into shape through their brilliance, experience, and know-how. However, Frontline Leadership work that is scalable, long-term, ingrained, and sustainable requires school leaders to honor, learn from, and amplify the voices and perspectives of a diverse community within and outside of a school building.

Frontline Leadership realizes that racially just and humanizing places bring people together, and school leaders see their own professional journey deeply tied to the success of the school and broader community. School leaders must pose tough questions, examine their own privileges, and move outside of what they may have always thought, what has worked for them in their own lives, and what has been done in the school previously. When necessary, in order to ensure racial justice, frontline leaders do not continue to carry forward traditional practices and policies that have done more harm than good in racially minoritized communities. This means that leaders in the fight for racial justice cultivate a leadership team of people who are focused on reimagining the vision and mission of a school and work with others to build spaces of humility and civility.

Perhaps most important, frontline leaders innovate and press toward the racially just ideal. Rather than conceiving the work of planning as an iterative process bound by historical, normative restraints, Frontline leaders enter ongoing design and planning processes dreaming, envisioning, and hoping for a community where Black students, Brown students, and other minoritized students feel a strong sense of belonging, want to be in and participate in the school, and experience schools that are safe, affirming, and healthy.

> Frontline leaders enter ongoing design and planning processes dreaming, envisioning, and hoping for a community where Black students, Brown students, and other minoritized students feel a strong sense of belonging, want to be in and participate in the school, and experience schools that are safe, affirming, and healthy.

Thus, planning and designing work insists that frontline leaders enter into community with colleges, Frontline Leadership team(s), and with ideal destinations of policies, practices, and outcomes that have perhaps never even been imagined or accomplished. It is the spirit of the possibility—the creativity and innovation of Frontline Leadership—that can create environments that make a difference in the lives of minoritized youth and communities.

To be clear, a school leader is not omniscient, omnipresent, or omnipotent. And school leaders, regardless of their experience, expertise, insights, commitments, and practices, should be careful not to present themselves as all-knowing or all-powerful. Instead, frontline leaders recognize that their capacity to succeed is necessarily connected to the lives, experiences, and contributions of others within and close to the community in which they are working. A school leader's capacity to build and cultivate a leadership team committed to racial equity and racial justice will allow them to co-create, co-plan, and co-design the kind of place where young people, faculty, and staff *desire* and *deserve* to be. Frontline leaders must deliberately and consistently answer several *probative* questions as they build a Frontline

Leadership team, a "dream team" of people unwavering and unapologetic in their commitment(s) toward racial justice:

- *Who should be involved in the leadership team?* Members of the leadership team should involve a wide and eclectically diverse group of people. To be sure, the school leader must be involved in the identification of these members and in the meetings and work of the collective. Perhaps more than any other stakeholder, young people (i.e., students) should be on the leadership team to help co-construct, draft, and revise vision and mission statements; identify blind spots; and recommend policies and practices. In addition, faculty and staff should be included along with community members outside of the school who live in the neighborhoods of the school or who have a vested interest in the school.

- *For how long should people (educators, young people, community members, families) serve and participate on a Frontline Leadership team?* The leadership team or collective will need to shift and alternate over time just as the situations, needs, challenges, issues, assets, and opportunities change. But there should always be rotating veteran Frontline Leadership members on the team. Frontline Leadership teams will need to be dynamic and evolving based on the social realities of the school, district, community, state, nation, and world. As faculty, staff, and students change, so too will the need to rotate and adjust the leadership team and the issues that penetrate the focus. For sure, the work of racial justice of the Frontline Leadership team cannot be seen as destination work. Rather, the vision, mission, policies, and practices must be as dynamic, fluid, evolving, and rotating as those who live in the school and world. What remains sternly and stubbornly consistent are core values related to disrupting racism, whiteness, and anti-Black racism.

- *How do school leaders decide on who should be involved on the Frontline Leadership team(s)?* Ideally, leadership teams consist of people, and especially racially minoritized individuals, who represent different areas (subject matter teachers, various grade-level instructors, clerical staff, custodial workers, lunchroom personnel) of a school, district, and community. An important point to remember in the work of constructing the team is people of color tend to be already engaging in mountains of invisible work related to racial equity. Rather than adding additional work and expectations to these educators' work, Frontline Leadership constructs an equitable framework to carry this work forward. This means that educators of color (as well as young people) are provided time off, course credit, and additional compensation for the emotionally and psychologically taxing additional work that is being asked of them. The work of the committee will and should vary. The point is not that clerical staff will have the same level of involvement as a social studies teacher, *per se*. However, all voices in the school will be important and should be considered, and communicating commitments to racial justice will remain essential. Stressing again, in all cases, student voices and participation in this work must be included. Others who might be considered and included on a Frontline Leadership team are school counselors, psychologists, staff members, teachers, caregivers, and broader community members.

- *How often should the Frontline Leadership team(s) meet?* If seen as a separate (marginal) group that is not really germane to the essence of success in the school or organization, the Frontline Leadership team will be seen as a group doing nonserious work ("good-hearted" people engaging in a hobby). However, if incorporated as a necessary cornerstone of all the work in a school, the Frontline Leadership collective will be seen as the most important group advancing the success of the social environment in alignment with the curriculum, instruction, assessment, and relationship practices. Frontline Leadership teams are constantly meeting, planning, designing, and strategizing to (1) identify and build on the most racially just policies and practice; (2) name, disrupt, and correct racism, whiteness, and anti-Black racism; (3) launch new initiatives; and (4) chart and expand unexplored racial justice territory.

- And perhaps most importantly, *what should the Frontline Leadership team(s) do?* This chapter is primarily focused on this question; that is, how do school leaders work with others in planning and designing racial justice work?

The preceding questions are those that frontline leaders must contemplate as they work to co-construct not only individual commitments, values, beliefs, mindsets, and practices but also ecosystems with people committed to the work of racial justice and equity.

Centering racial justice and equity, Frontline Leadership team members work collectively to (a) construct, refine, revise, and advance vision and mission; (b) collect data—that is, survey, communicate with, and gauge individual and collective challenges and success; (c) be advisory to leadership; (d) design and develop professional learning opportunities for and with faculty, staff, students, and broader communities; and (e) learn about, build knowledge about, understand, and interpret district, state, and national policies that have a bearing on the racial health of a school environment. Ideally, this work is not seen as "extra" or tangential to the real work of the school. On the contrary, ideally, members of the Frontline Leadership team, particularly those of color, should be compensated with relevant forms of capital to maximize potential expertise and contributions. If Frontline Leadership is seen from a perspective of equity, there will be few questions about compensation structures for those communities of color that labor behind the scenes to create and maintain powerfully rigorous, affirming, and transformative spaces. In other words, Frontline Leadership collectives are more beneficial when they are integrated as part of the fabric of schoolwork and learning rather than an add-on to or an afterthought to the work that really matters.

Frontline leaders must be learners. They must build knowledge, based on research and well-established evidence, to advocate for the teachers, students, and communities in which they serve. They must not only learn and build knowledge, but frontline leaders must also build deep understandings about complex issues we face in education along with solutions to address challenges. Frontline leaders' learning, knowing, and understanding require that they are not only focused on their local school and district. These leaders committed to disrupting racism, whiteness, and anti-Black racism must learn, know, and understand how macro (societal), meso (district), and school (micro) level issues impact their work in education. These intersecting units of analysis (macro, meso, micro) allow school leaders to build a powerful toolkit—a repository of insights that are relevant to, responsive for, and well aligned with goals and visions of their local district and school. Figure 1.1 (from Chapter 1) provides a powerful snapshot of the kinds of focal areas that every school leader committed to racial justice must consider. Perhaps most importantly, school leaders must co-construct an ecological context where an anti-racist ethos permeates entire school buildings and classrooms. This means that frontline leaders are curating curriculum sites that build on standards while simultaneously responding to societal realities.

In this way, curriculum design takes into consideration the ideal for and with racial minoritized students and communities. Frontline leaders study, understand, and are intentional about (a) what students have the opportunity to learn about racial justice on the walls in a school building; (b) who greets students in the mornings; (c) who teaches students (hiring); (d) what schoolwide themes and community readings are required and expected in classrooms and the entire school; and (e) how, when, and where adults speak out about issues of racial justice and racial oppression inside and outside of school. Frontline Leadership conceives of and accepts responsibility for the professional learning of educators in the space. Such responsibility requires that they read about and amplify policies, discourses, and practices designed to disrupt racial justice. In this way, planning and designing as sites of curriculum can manifest as spaces for learning and development throughout a school based on societal racialized realities.

Some may believe the issues outlined at the end of the previous paragraph are tangential to, not salient for, or irrelevant in the kinds of learning opportunities educators and young people should engage in in schools to learn and grow. But if we view the issues as learning opportunities that students are *already* learning about simply by living in society, schools are neglecting opportunities to help prepare them for the real world in which they are currently living. Thus, frontline leaders know that they should be actively involved with planning and designing learning opportunities to help students build necessary skills to analyze, critique, and understand what is happening in society, why these situations happen, and perhaps what can be done about it. (See my discussion of the curriculum as a site of social action in Chapter 2.) In this way, frontline leaders are always mindful of developmental appropriateness for work of racial justice and are astutely planning and designing opportunities for deep learning over time and space.

If we have a fighting chance of disrupting pervasive patterns that dehumanize and marginalize, frontline leaders must step up and support the next generation of young people in creating a more racially just world. Indeed, we cannot assume that adults in schools (teachers, counselors, social workers, school resource officers, staff, and school leaders) have the knowledge and overall commitment to disrupting racial injustice and inequity. Frontline Leadership sets the motivational, innovative, creative, and otherwise passion for what might be possible in planning and designing.

The What and How of Collective Work

The work of a frontline leader requires much attention to race, racism, whiteness, and anti-Black racism. In the case of developing systems and practices that pursue and realize racial justice, frontline leaders must be deliberate about identifying and supporting Frontline Leadership teams' progress (at the right time) as they are committed to the morale, confidence, knowledge, and practices of staff, faculty, students, families, and the broader neighborhood community.

Frontline leaders understand and advance the reality that the foundation and premise of dialogue and action among leadership team members are fueled for, by, and through data collection. In other words, as leaders and leadership work to advance racial justice and racial equity, they must do so through developing and enacting data collection strategies, tools, and cycles designed to shape who participates in a leadership collective, when they participate, for how long, what the focus of the work will/should/must be, and what actionable steps are needed to pursue racial justice and equity. Thus, framing categories (see bullet list) are shaped by a full commitment and desire to make decisions based on data.

By data, I do not mean that the Frontline Leadership collectives are charged with developing, implementing, and interpreting full research projects. Rather, what I have learned is that data (i.e., stories, themes, and/or patterns that emerge from a *systematic way of learning and knowing* about issues) allow racially justice minded individuals and groups to build recommendations, initiative, strategies, policies, practices, and action steps that are grounded in, shaped by, and steeped in what is known from a systematic way of learning and knowing. I have also found that those in a school and community (faculty, staff, young people, families, and community members) are more open to suggested change, reform, and transformation when data are used to anchor and launch policies and practices for racial justice. Moreover, data collection should be designed and implemented as an opportunity to *probe*—to determine challenges schools, organizations, and communities face but also to document the many established and developing successes and assets of a system, structure, organization, or ecological system. In short and sum, by data collection, I mean the deliberate planning and designing of mechanisms, tools, and strategies *to know more to do better.* Rather than framing these moves, interactions, and learning opportunities as data collection, I am calling them *probing* actions that require deep introspection, cognitive care, and attention to design with fidelity. These probes have potential for long-term, sustained, and scaled benefit and affordances. As frontline leaders plan and design in collaboration with a leadership collective, leaders are planning and designing opportunities that address and advance the interconnectedness among the following areas:

> Those in a school and community (faculty, staff, young people, families, and community members) are more open to suggested change, reform, and transformation when data are used to anchor and launch policies and practices for racial justice.

- *Ecological and Environmental Probing.* Frontline leaders recognize that the broader ethos of the school and community—the culture of the place and space—must be a major priority. Leaders invite, encourage, and help those on the leadership team build tools to gain a pulse on how things are going in the school or organization. How are people doing (the affective and feeling)? What do people *think or believe* about the racial justice work (not) happening (cognitive and intellectual)?[i] What are people (not) doing to advance racial justice and equity (behavioral, practice, and action)? How are people treating each other (social, interactional, relational)? How are racist people and racist actions being addressed in the place (affective, cognitive, and behavioral)? What types of professional learning are essential to co-create spaces of racial liberation, wellness, and transformation?

- *Curriculum Probing.* Frontline leaders understand that state- and district-level curricula may fall way short of addressing racism, whiteness, anti-Black racism, as well as other forms of oppression. This means that the curriculum cannot be seen as a static document, graded course of study, or a curriculum guide that educators follow as if they were robots themselves and teaching robots. Rather, Frontline Leadership through collective partnership determines the degree to which the curriculum adds value to the racialized lives, knowledge, understanding, and humanity of students with whom it is co-designed. In an era when educators are being told what the curriculum is and should be regarding racial equity, data-driven decisions are essential in the fight for racial justice. What is being offered in the curriculum that cultivates spaces for young people to interrogate racism, xenophobia, and other forms of discrimination? What curriculum shifts and transformations are necessary for racial identity development, racial affirmation, and racial community contributions? To what degree is the curriculum designed to be transformative and to cultivate social action among young people? (See Chapter 2 for more on the idea of pushing the curriculum to transformation levels and social action levels for racial justice.) What types of supports do teachers and other educators in the space need to design and enact racially just curriculum practices?

- *Instructional Probing.* Frontline collectives also have the opportunity and responsibility to identify when effective, opportunity-centered teaching is happening and when teaching

---

[i]By cognitive demand, I mean educators are reflecting on the deep and heavy thinking that is required to locate and understand their own established beliefs and thoughts as new and more challenging insights are being introduced and expectations expand.

needs to change. Instructional probing is about mapping the extent to which young people are learning the curriculum through pedagogical decisions from educators. How are educators building instructional opportunities that bring the curriculum to life for racially minoritized communities? What instructional moves do educators make to push the curriculum beyond basic, rote memorization? What instructional skills do teachers exhibit that help students push beyond lower-level analyses of a text in literature or social studies about race and racism, for instance, to critical consciousness that invites students to pose deeper questions about racial inequity and join a collective fight against *-isms* and *-phobias*? How do teachers build instructional practices that cultivate social action?

- *Psychological, Mental Health, Emotional, and Affective Probing.* Educators, families, parents, and communities are pressing to learn more about what is necessary to build communities of wellness, those in which students, faculty, staff, family members, and broader community members feel psychologically, mentally, emotionally, and affectively healthy. Indeed, young people may be experiencing psychological strain because they are or have been (as traumatic experiences can linger) experiencing racism. Studying how minoritized people (young people, staff, faculty) are doing is essential as we work to address not only the academic needs of students but also their mental wellness in a broader society pushing to further dehumanize communities of color. Focusing on the adults who work with students is just as important as centering young people because people who are hurting can hurt and traumatize others.

- *Behavioral Probing.* Frontline Leadership teams also must observe and capture what they see, just as they are appropriately listening to those in the community. To what degree is there a disconnect between what adults or young people are saying about their commitment to racial justice and what is observable in their practices? Indeed, there should be deliberate synergy between talking and doing, and behavioral probing insists that there is consistency between discourse and action. Similarly, there are important opportunities to probe connections between what is observed in actionable practices and what is said. For instance, do you observe increases in, consistency around, or changes in the (a) over-referral of Black students to the office, (b) a disproportionate number of Black students who are suspended and expelled, (c) an overwhelming and disproportionate number of Black students who are referred to special education for behavioral challenges, and/or (d) under-referral of Black and other racialized minoritized students to gifted and advanced placement? When these rates change, we have evidence of behavioral shifts among adults that are also powerful indicators of the broader ethos of a space committed to inclusivity, justice, opportunity, and joy. In other words, behavioral shifts are made visible when disproportionality rates and other outcomes negatively affecting communities of color decline.

- *Assessment Probing.* Although often taken for granted beyond standardized exams, assessments are a necessary equity and justice site for probing and inquiring because the assessments help educators understand what they have taught, what they need to teach or reteach, and how their students are faring. If designed effectively, assessments would not only focus on academic tasks such as what mathematical or scientific learning has taken place over a given time. Instead, assessments will also zone in on the other important aspects of human experience such as mental health growth and development, feelings and sense of belonging, and hiring practices to increase educators and staff of color. Just as young people and teachers are being assessed, so too must frontline leaders on metrics that build safe and affirming contexts. Assessments should be viewed as a mechanism to gauge classroom-level matters as well as broader school, community, and district successes, challenges, and realities. Assessments can help the leadership teams determine when and if young people experience blatant and more subtle forms of racism. In this way, Frontline Leadership teams should be assessing the assessments in our fight to disrupt racism, whiteness, and anti-Black racism. For instance, are the assessments racially biased? Are assessments offered in multiple languages? Are students given the option to complete assessments, such as a writing task, using multiple languages? How are assessments designed to be racially and culturally responsive?

Taken together, the areas of emphasis in Table 3.1 have the potential to help frontline leaders build systems, organizations, structures, initiatives, and institutions necessary to co-create and co-design racially just spaces and places.

Understanding Self as a Precursor for Designing and Planning

For frontline leaders, understanding, building knowledge about, and advancing racial justice work involves critical race self-reflection. In the

TABLE 3.1 Probing Practices for Racial Justice		
FOCAL AREA	**DESCRIPTION**	**WHAT MATTERS**
Ecological and Social Probing	Study the culture of the place and space. Centering racial equity, how are people feeling in the community? What do people think or believe about the racial justice work (not) happening in the environment? What are people doing to advance racial justice and equity work in the school?	Social context of the school and classroom
Curriculum Probing	Examine how curriculum practices add value to the racialized lives, knowledge, understanding, and humanity of the students with whom the curriculum is designed.	What students learn and what adults emphasize as essential to know and be able to do
Instructional Probing	Map the extent to which young people are learning the curriculum through pedagogical decisions from educators. How are educators building instructional opportunities that bring race, racism, and discrimination to life through the curriculum?	How educators understand, interpret, and enact the curriculum What teachers teach
Psychological, Mental Health, Emotional, and Affective Probing	Probe into the ways in which the school itself, through its racist origins, practices, and policies, may contribute to psychological, emotional, and traumatic experiences of young people and adults.	Individual and collective well-being of adults and young people
Behavioral Probing	Study the degree to which there is a disconnect between what adults or young people are saying about their commitment to racial justice and what is observable in their practices. Indeed, there should be deliberate synergy between talking and doing, and behavioral probing insists that there is consistency between discourse and action.	What people do in place and space, when, and how
Assessment Probing	Identify mechanisms that support improvement. Especially for racial minoritized people, assessments have been used to dehumanize them, and they have been used as weapons to cause harm to individuals and communities.	How adults and young people are evaluated, rewarded, and supported to improve

work of anti-racist leadership, critical race theorists (cf. Ladson-Billings & Tate, 1995) and other racially and culturally sensitive researchers and theorists (Tillman, 2002) demonstrate how (and why) we need to critique past and current situations to change and transform our world moving forward. For sure, if we are to avoid (or at best combat) a race war (as described in Chapter 1), we must understand and name the United States' racist past to avoid repeating it. This introspection allows frontline leaders to think about what they feel (affective) and believe (cognitive) about the past and understand their own roles in racial inequity. Engaging in deep, introspective questions about race can bring to leaders' awareness and consciousness known (seen), unknown (unseen), and unanticipated (unforeseen) issues, perspectives, positions, and behaviors that they may not have considered otherwise (Milner, 2007). Through reflection, *seen* areas are those that can become apparent to a frontline leader based on explicit behaviors or feedback from others. *Unforeseen* areas are those spaces where frontline leaders make decisions that they could have never predicted or anticipated could cause harm to others. And *unseen* areas of introspection focus on issues, practices, and potential outcomes that prove invisible to school leaders. Although the work of introspection is important for school leaders across racial backgrounds, this work of reflection is especially essential for white educators. I expand with examples of how such introspection may manifest.

> A *seen reflective* issue, perspective, position, or behavior may occur when a school leader hires mostly white educators (even in a pool of more racially diverse candidates) because the school leader perceives these white educators are more qualified than candidates of color. Feedback, complaints, and challenges the leader receives about the low number of teachers of color in classrooms and schools, the racial disconnects these students have with their teachers, and the racism students of color experience from some of their white teachers provide space for a seen decision that, retrospectively, seemed to have done more harm than good, at least for young people of color.

> An *unforeseen reflective* issue, perspective, position, or behavior may be when a school leader decides to allow an underinformed or underprepared educator of color to lead a student group who ostracizes, belittles, and reprimands students of color for not working hard enough or not working as hard as the white students in the school. This decision of the frontline leader, albeit unintentional, is an unforeseen (that is, unpredictable) leadership decision that could leave students of color with lasting scars and psychological strain.

> An *unseen reflective* issue, perspective, position, or behavior could occur when a school leader selects a schoolwide reading or supports the requirement of a reading for all students about slavery, Chinese internment camps, or the Holocaust, and educators teaching the book are underprepared for the questions, insensitive comments, and emotional strain among the racial and ethnic minoritized students. A school leader may not see how students of color feel embarrassed,

stressed, or frustrated by both the content of the book and
educators' inability to guide discussions about and disrupt
underinformed views about the historical genesis of these
ideas as they relate to and connect to current ones.

Understandably (and unfortunately), some leaders may recognize
the importance of racial introspection but may not know where to
begin. Leaders may not understand the need to engage in reflection,
especially those leaders who historically have adopted color-blind,
race-avoidant ideologies, beliefs, attitudes, and practices. Indeed,
West (1993) explained that it is difficult to work for emancipation on
behalf of others (and to work to solve problems with and on behalf
of others) until people (or, in this case, leaders) are free themselves.
Thus, reflection allows frontline leaders to think about the ways in
which seen, unforeseen, and unseen decisions can have serious effects
on human development.

Dillard (2000) found that each time people engage in reflection, they are
re-searching themselves all over again. Several questions for frontline
leaders may prove helpful in the process of building more robust racially
just and equitable practices. I recommend the following guided questions
for frontline leaders as necessary in planning and designing spaces of
justice and equity:

- What is my racial background? How do I know?

- What is my family's story about race? That is, how did my family
  interact with, talk about, engage, and work with families outside of
  our racial background? How do I know?

- In what ways might my race influence how I experience the world,
  what I emphasize in my leadership and educational practices, and
  how I evaluate and interpret others and their experiences? How
  do I know?

- How do I understand my own privileges (educational, gendered,
  sexual, socioeconomic) in classrooms, schools, districts, and the
  broader society? How do these privileges *intersect with or diverge
  from* my racial identity?

- Particularly for white school leaders, what (if anything)
  am I willing to give up to benefit the collective humanity of
  communities of color?

- What do I feel, know, and believe about the role of race, racism,
  oppression, and white supremacy in society and education?

- How have I come to understand the role of race and racism in my own work and my own life?

- What are and have been the contextual nuances and realities that help shape my racialized ways of understanding policies, practices, and other people's experiences and behaviors?

- What racialized experiences have shaped my personal and professional decisions, practices, approaches, agendas, life, and work? How do these personal and professional moves intersect and diverge, and what do these lessons tell one about my leadership?

As hooks (1994) explained, educators must work to advance practices where they are working to improve themselves just as they are working to support student development. In this way, educators employ a "holistic model of learning . . . where [leaders] grow" (p. 21) and know more about themselves as they support the health and vitality of the school environment. Frontline Leadership is not separate from the reality of the world and school, and frontline leaders demystify the power structure and share power and decision making with others with whom they are working. Frontline leaders are constantly reflecting and becoming more cognizant of who they are and why they believe what they do.

Indeed, deep introspective work is required of frontline leaders when they are committed to improving their school communities by including racial justice in their agendas and platforms.

Partnering With Families as Racial Justice Warriors

Particularly for educators working in early and elementary education, they have a chance to set the course for how families imagine school and family connections for years to come. As a parent, I know that I am doing the very best I can to support my children for school success. But, even as a university professor of education, I still experience a deep level of anxiety and vulnerability as I attempt to partner with educators to support my children. As I have communicated with other families (Milner, 2020d; Milner et al., 2018), I have learned that they too yearn for opportunities to build stronger partnerships with educators. For families and caregivers of color, engaging with families about their children can be even more taxing. Thus, Frontline Leadership embraces the challenge of including families (parents and caregivers) in the designing and planning of racial justice work. But to build the kinds of relationships with parents to be successful, frontline leaders understand that their communication patterns and interactional styles must be keenly in place, particularly when communities of color are rebounding from *fractured relationships* with schools—their children's teachers and school leaders.

I recall sitting and observing nurses and doctors when my father-in-law was hospitalized for treatments related to cancer of the pancreas. Although the messaging of his situation was obviously devastating, the way those professionals communicated with him about his condition and the treatment plan was nothing short of gracious, respectful, trusting, hopeful, empathetic, and caring. My father-in-law and our family, although concerned about his health, were made to feel like we mattered. The doctors and nurses seemed to understand the art and science of bedside manner and its potential impact for our family. As educators design initial and subsequent interactions with families that demonstrate trust, collaboration, and advocacy, they have a better chance of effectively meeting the needs of students. Not to pathologize the needs of young people, I believe frontline leaders and other educators can learn something significant about how to communicate with families and build lasting partnerships with them. As teachers prepare to build and cultivate positive, relevant, and meaningful partnerships and collaborations with families in the design and planning of opportunities that work against racism, whiteness, and anti-Black racism, I offer the following six recommendations:

1. ***Stress the Importance of Working Together.*** It is essential for frontline leaders to *explicitly share* that you are all on the same "team" as families, parents, and school learn to do better in the work of racial justice. Families need to know that school leadership is working *with, for,* and *not against* them to support their children. Because some caregivers (and too many families of color) have had negative experiences in schools as students themselves and/or with previous educators of their children, they may need to be reassured that frontline leaders are not working "against" them but rather *with them* to support their children to repair fractured school–family relationships. In this sense, teachers cannot assume that family members know (or believe) that schools are on their side in the education of their children.

2. ***Acknowledge Families and Parents as Knowers.*** If families are going to become an essential partner in the work of equity in the school, frontline leaders must value, validate, and demonstrate appreciation for the vast, deep, and robust knowledge, awareness, expertise, and insights caregivers have and are willing to share. Although educators can rely on their past

experiences as teachers, as former students, and/or as parents, it is necessary for them to also acknowledge that families and parents are indeed knowledgeable about their children. Frontline leaders do not act as the only knowers in the place. Using unknown acronyms and loaded academic jargon can turn caregivers off and can damage potential racial justice collaboration and partnership. Frontline Leadership expects, allows, and encourages families and parents to be "experts" on their children's experiences. Despite what school leaders might believe they know about young people in their school, family members have a deep knowledge of their children (e.g., their history, their preferences, their challenges, and their assets) that must be used to bridge the relational capacity necessary for a partnership of racial justice.

3. *Identify and Articulate Student Strengths.* Rather than waiting until there is a concern to report, like teachers, frontline leaders facilitate ways to identify and communicate to caregivers observed assets of students. For many families of color, the only time they communicate with school leaders (especially assistant principals and principals) is when something negative has happened or when there is a concern about children. Imagine the deep level of admiration and appreciation families would have for school leaders who take the time to communicate strengths, appreciation, and admiration of young people to their families. Such communication tightens the potential bond between frontline leaders and families. Frontline leaders focus on and articulate, orally and in writing, assets and potential that they observe in young people. In education, we tend to focus on what young people do not know and then try to "fill in the gap." A different approach is to identify assets of young people and build on them instead.

4. *Express Commitment to Development.* As frontline leaders are communicating with families, they express that young people develop different skills at different times of learning and development. Share with families that it is the school's role to help students develop and help ease families' anxieties when their children are not developing a particular desired skill at the same rate as others or even a desired pace. Even as frontline leaders provide recommendations, these leaders express to families the belief in educators in the school to work with them as caregivers to reach desirable goals and expectations. Young people, like all of us, are and should be viewed as developing beings, and frontline leaders can model such commitment for educators in the school by communicating the necessary role of development. To be sure,

families of color are too often talked about as inadequate, behind, and deficient. If frontline leaders want to partner with families toward racial justice, young people have to be viewed as those who are developing (and will develop) over time.

5. ***Demystify the Educational Process.*** Most of the time, families are doing the very best that they can to support their young people. Families do not want to feel like they are poorly parenting and supporting their children, just as educators do not want to feel that they are not effective. One way of helping to ease tension and worry among families is for frontline leaders to model, share, and encourage other educators to express personal anecdotes with families about challenges they personally had with young people in their own family (sons, daughters, nieces, nephews). The sharing of personal challenges in children's learning, development, and education provides a space for families to understand that children from different walks of life, even the children of educators, may have challenges. The sharing of these stories can bridge implicit divisions between educators and caregivers because families start to see frontline leaders and other educators as real people and consequently may believe educators are not judging them. Concurrently, the sharing of successes—and particularly how families worked through and overcame challenges—can be motivational and a connective tissue between schools and families.

6. ***Set Agreeable Forms of Communication.*** Because frontline leaders are asking for the time and expertise of families in the partnership toward racial justice, knowing the best means of communication for families is essential. As technology becomes more sophisticated each day, frontline leaders query families about their preferred forms of communication. Investigate established technology tools available, and engage with educators about communication trends they have found throughout their work and careers. Knowing whether families are more (or less) responsive to particular kinds of communication can help facilitate more seamless interactions and advance the work against racism, whiteness, and anti-Black racism.

Table 3.2 captures these essential elements that I hope frontline leaders use in professional learning opportunities. Indeed, throughout this book, in addition to connecting with, validating, and learning from families, parents, and caregivers, I have stressed the importance of engaging young people in the work of planning and designing schools for racial

TABLE 3.2　Partnerships to Cultivate Racial Justice Collaborations With Families, Parents, and Caregivers	
PARTNERSHIP PRACTICE FOR RACIAL JUSTICE	**LEADERSHIP MOVES**
Stress the Importance of Working Together.	Frontline leaders *explicitly share* that you are all on the same "team" as families, parents, and schools learn to do better in the work of racial justice.
Acknowledge Families and Parents as Knowers.	Frontline leaders value, validate, and demonstrate appreciation for the vast, deep, and robust knowledge, awareness, expertise, and insights caregivers have and are willing to share.
Identify and Articulate Student Strengths.	Frontline leaders facilitate ways to identify and communicate to caregivers observed assets and potential of students.
Express Commitment to Development.	Frontline leaders express that young people develop different skills at different times of learning and development.
Demystify the Educational Process.	Frontline leaders model, share, and encourage other educators to express personal anecdotes with families about challenges and successes they personally have had in schools.
Set Agreeable Forms of Communication.	Frontline leaders query families about their preferred forms of communication.

justice work in time, place, and space. But what does student engagement mean in schools, where the focus is not only what happens inside a classroom? Moreover, what do frontline leaders need to know and be able to do to support, learn from, and engage young people in this arduous task of co-designing spaces of racial justice?

Student Engagement in Racial Justice Work

Student engagement has been defined as the "attention, interest, investment, and effort students expend in the work of learning" (Marks, 2000, p. 155). It has also been conceptualized as students' involvement with their school, their investment in and effort applied in learning, understanding, or mastering the knowledge, skills, or practices that promote development (Newmann et al., 1992), and students' motivation to do their work. Doyle (1983) and Woolfolk (1998) relate student engagement to "engaged time"—the time educators (and I would add frontline leaders) and students spend actively involved in specific tasks toward specific ends. Essentially, student engagement concerns the interests, efforts, and connections students display in a school environment. Engaging young people in racial justice work means that frontline leaders become actively connected to students, develop a school curriculum inclusive of and beyond what happens in classrooms, and help develop young people's knowledge, understanding, insights, and skillsets related to contribution of racial justice and equity.

Freire's (1998) work is primarily concerned with using education as the practice of freedom. In other words, the major purpose of education in Freire's assessment is freedom that is connected to deep understandings of self, society, and human life experiences. Freire encourages simultaneous reflection on self and the world to uncover inconspicuous and deeply hidden phenomena. He contends that "authentic reflection considers neither abstract [person/people] nor the world without people, but people in their relations with the world. In these relations, consciousness and world are simultaneous: consciousness neither precedes the world nor follows it" (Freire, 1998, p. 62). When this reflection occurs, adults and young people alike reflect authentically on past experiences beyond the walls of academia. Both groups ask themselves, "Why do I believe what I believe?" and work together to find answers and solutions. Engagement of young people in racial justice work requires that they focus on themselves and the broader world and communities in which they live. In Freire's (1998) words, "As [people], simultaneously reflecting on themselves and the world, increase the scope of their perceptions, they begin to direct their observations towards previously inconspicuous phenomena" (p. 63). Students and young people ask, What has happened to me in the world that influences my thinking and positions inside of the school? Thus, engaging young people in racial justice work requires leadership that shepherds them into places where they examine what guides, frames, and shapes their worldviews. This examination will influence their critiques and recommendations about what is, is not, and should happen to increase racial justice in schools.

Studying and Connecting to the Real World

Freire (1998) discussed the importance of people studying and connecting to real-world phenomena in pursuit of liberation. This principle asks young people and adults to answer an important question: How do I understand, connect, and situate what is happening in the broader world with what is occurring in school? For potentially transformative interactions with young people, adults must ponder whether they believe their own knowledge and expertise are superior to the knowledge and expertise of students. In short, we know and understand life, politics, and school-related phenomena through our experiences, worldviews, values, privileges, and challenges in and of the world. So, helping students make cognitive connections will be necessary for young people to develop insights that can advance racial justice work in schools. Rather than viewing their knowledge as superior to their students, frontline leaders and other adults in a school must amplify, value, and validate student experiences and work as agents with students (some of whom have been historically oppressed) in pursuit of their individual and collective emancipation. As a result, the engagement of young people in the work of racial justice can lead to education as a practice of freedom (Freire, 1998).

As Freire (1998) stressed, education with oppressed communities must be forged with, not for, the oppressed (whether individuals or peoples) in the struggle to regain and capture their emancipated place in schools and in society. It is important to note that Frontline Leadership does not work to reinforce binaries where people are determined to be one, singular, myopic being or another. Rather, Frontline Leadership acknowledges that oppression exists and that people can experience the world as an oppressed being in one aspect of their life and as a privileged being in another.

> The engagement of young people in the work of racial justice can lead to education as a practice of freedom (Freire, 1998).

In the work of racial justice and the engagement of young people, freedom must be pursued constantly and responsibly. To be clear, too many young people operate in oppressive schooling communities. Including them in transforming and building a more humanizing context with communities of color will require deeply deliberate and careful work.

This engagement through leadership practices is important to avoid further traumatizing students as they reflect on past racist experiences they have had. Freire (1998) wrote, "Freedom is not an ideal located outside of [people]; nor is it an idea, which becomes myth. It is rather the indispensable condition for the quest for human completion" (p. 29). The engagement of students in improving a school community has the potential to help them live in more complete and humanizing ways in the world. Indeed, young people and educators must understand that, even as they are working to improve the school community, they operate in and through power structures. These power structures tend to be unlike the levels of power differentials that adults experience with each other, even among school leaders and educators and staff. Young people working with adults on these issues of racial justice necessitate an even greater awareness of how power can be a deterrent to the kinds of transformation needed to work against racism, whiteness, and anti-Black racism.

Awareness of and
Understanding Power Structures

As young people are engaging in racial justice work, it is important for them to be positioned as real participants in the thinking, decision-making, planning, and designing work of racial justice. In preparing and supporting the engagement of young people in racial justice work, Freire (1998) wrote about the need to move away from a banking model and approach, in which educators see their role in education as "an act of depositing, in which the students are the depositories and the [leader] is the depositor" (p. 53). Perhaps more so than in a classroom, rejecting a banking approach in racial justice work of a school, Freire supports an education process with young people that is problem-posing. This means that school leaders reject a top-down developmental process where they make deposits "which the students patiently receive, memorize, and repeat" (Freire, 1998, p. 53). This point is especially important because individuals, whether adults or students, are the experts on and about their experiences. Frontline leaders, then, will need to work in collaboration with young people, listening to their experiences as decisions are made to improve the school community. Frontline Leadership insists that leaders understand various levels of power. Delpit (1995) described five aspects of power:

> To be clear, too many young people operate in oppressive schooling communities. Including them in transforming and building a more humanizing context with communities of color will require deeply deliberate and careful work.

> (a) Issues of power are enacted in classroom [and schools];
> (b) there are codes or rules for participating in power; that is, there is a "culture of power"; (c) the rules of the culture of power are a reflection of the rules of the culture of those who have power; (d) if you are not already a participant in the culture of power, being told explicitly the rules of that culture makes acquiring power easier; and (e) those with power are frequently least aware of—or least willing to acknowledge—its existence. Those with less power are often most aware of its existence. (p. 24)

Thus, frontline leaders are engaging young people in planning for and designing questions that bring out, connect with, and tap into student interests, experiences, troubles, and assets to negotiate a power structure that may be difficult for young people to work through because they have mostly interacted with school leaders as the people in charge and holding all the questions, answers, and insights. Through problem-posing education, young people develop their own power to perceive "critically the way they exist in the world with which and in which they find themselves; they come to see the world not as a static reality, but as a reality of process, in transformation" (Freire, 1998, p. 64). Stressing self-perception, problem-posing education bases its philosophy in creativity and stimulates true reflection and action upon reality. Problem-posing education plans and designs places with young people to decide what is needed in their lives at school to create strong connections to the curriculum, instruction, assessment, and relational practices in a school.

Freire further explained that educators who support the banking concept of education perceive their work in the following way:

> Knowledge is a gift bestowed by those who consider themselves knowledgeable upon those whom they consider to know nothing. Projecting an absolute ignorance onto others, a characteristic of the ideology of oppression, negates education and knowledge as processes of inquiry. . . . The students, alienated like the slave . . . accept their ignorance as justifying the [educator's] existence—but, unlike the slave; they never discover that they educate the [school leader and other educators]. (Freire, 1998, p. 53)

Accordingly, frontline leaders pose important questions about power and how power structures are reified to maintain an inequitable status quo, even as they pretend to bring in young people as agents to help a school get better.

- Is my role as school leader superior to the experiences and expertise of students?

- What knowledge must I learn from the students with whom I work to make the school, neighborhood, and community better?

- How do I co-construct spaces where young people feel confident enough to engage with me given power structures and divisions between school leaders and young people?

Students themselves should be posing similar questions introspectively and in community with adults who may disagree, be offended, or who do not understand their experiences (particularly when leaders are white and young people are of color).

Back to the Power of Talk

Engaging young people in substantive, sustained, and sustainable ways requires building their confidence and capacity to talk with adults who they may see as intimidating, unwelcoming, or even traumatizing. This means that developing agreements and tools for how young people voice their views will be necessary. Three important questions for leaders to ponder include (a) How do I situate myself politically? (b) Am I willing to speak on behalf of those [young people and other minoritized/oppressed groups] who might not *yet* be able to or feel comfortable enough to speak for themselves in a room with adults? (c) To what degree am I willing and able to speak for students when they are not present in the room? (d) What role do I play in co-developing a space where young people's talk is compelling, their voices are heard, and their perspectives meaningfully show up in challenging the school's culture and in identifying solutions for racial justice in schools?

Especially when considering the possibility of truly engaging young people in planning and designing tools, practices, frameworks, and initiatives for racial justice, frontline leaders must recognize and discuss with young people the ominous implications and responsibilities of talk with adults. Moreover, young people must understand and embrace the notion that when individuals speak, they are acting and thus being political. Frontline Leadership is necessarily political. Young people must understand that their sharing is guided by a set of values, assumptions, and beliefs that are carried forward as politically charged rhetoric. Thus, young people must be guided to engage in thoughtful and deliberate introspection as they share their views and perspectives with others. Part of the challenge of careful sharing is the potential backlash, repercussions, and disappointment from educators as young people of color tell the truth about the racist school, including the racist, white, and anti-Black curriculum; the racist, white, and anti-Black instruction; the racist, white, and anti-Black assessment; and the racist, white, and anti-Black relational practices.

Freire stressed the importance of reflecting before speaking, as reflection helps to advance potentially transformative actions. Freire (1998) lamented:

> Within the word we find two dimensions, reflection and action, in such radical interaction that if one is sacrificed— even in part—the other immediately suffers. There is no true word that is not at the same time praxis. Thus to speak a true word is to transform the world . . . it becomes an empty word, one which cannot denounce the world, for denunciation is

impossible without a commitment to transform, and there is no transformation without action. (p. 68)

When individuals speak, they take positions on issues and often-controversial topics, and they have an opportunity to transform the world through the spoken word. Because discourse is powerful, it is imperative for individuals to reflect before speaking. Frontline leaders design and plan for what happens when discourse is neglected, unheard, or ignored. When individuals speak truth to power, others may be challenged, even offended. And young people must be protected, on all levels, if they are going to be invited to participate in racial justice work to improve the school. Thus, it is already a huge, unfair requirement and expectation that young people have to be chiefly involved in helping adults get it right, and young people should be celebrated, not ostracized, for speaking their truth. Indeed, Freire reminded us that true discourse is a practice of freedom. He stressed the importance of genuine, authentic reflection in pursuit of education on behalf of all people (including young people), not just a select few (adults). Thus, young people must be prepared and supported for intense debate and discourse, particularly since we have a difficult time engaging in conversations about racism, whiteness, and anti-Black racism in society and especially in schools.

Designing and Planning as a Frontline Leader and in a Team

Frontline leaders understand and acknowledge that racial justice work does not just happen by chance. Leaders may have good intentions, but if they are not working carefully with colleagues to build Frontline Leadership collectives and capacity, it will be difficult to capitalize on visions and missions designed to disrupt inequitable, racist policies and practices. Frontline Leadership requires intentional planning and designing that thoughtfully engineers a context that supports other leaders, staff, faculty, and young people in their quests to do what is necessary for racial justice in classrooms, schools, and districts.

Designing and Planning to Actualize Visions and Missions

I adopt and adapt findings from important research on educator planning to shed light on essential elements of Frontline Leadership design and planning to move individual and collective racial justice efforts forward. To be clear, leaders must be steadfast in their desires and designs to support and build systems and communities dedicated to learning. Young people and adults need to recognize where they are in their racial justice journey. Designing and planning for racial justice and racial equity, then, insists that the entire community must start where they are but not stay there (Milner, 2020).

Preactive Planning: Planning Before Implementation

Much of educator planning that leads to design features is done mentally, that is, in educators' heads. Jackson (1968) served as a forerunner in the research on educator planning. He identified qualitatively cognitive and conceptual differences in the planning of educators before (preactive), during (interactive), and after (postactive or reflective) classroom interaction. *Preactive planning* concerns educator planning before they teach, execute a task, or implement a strategy. The planning of educators in the preactive phase may be mentally constructed, but the basic idea behind preactive planning focuses on the organizing and preparation that educators do in foresight of the actual actions they wish to see come to fruition. Research has shown that educators may write down only sketchy preactive plans or notes when compared to their more expansive mental models. In this sense, frontline leaders think carefully about the work they (and their collective) envision. As leaders are designing and planning for racial justice, they engage in preactive work where they not only think about and mentally plan to advance curriculum, instructional, assessment, and relational practices but also write and sketch outlines for the work ahead. Because leaders move from one school to the next, writing out some dimensions of preactive planning is necessary because the living documents allow new leadership to examine, build on, refine, revise, reject, and adapt plans as their own leadership shifts. Thus, Frontline Leadership constructs preactive documents that live in a repository to assist the next school leadership team.

Interactive Planning: Planning While Implementing

In addition to planning before practice (preactive planning), educators must also plan during the implementation of racial justice work. *Interactive planning* concerns the planning of educators while they are moving the work forward, that is, while they are doing racial justice and racial equity work. In other words, designing and planning are necessary while policies and practices are enacted. For instance, during professional development about race, racism, and anti-Black racism, leaders are planning (largely mentally) while they are carrying out learning and development opportunities with faculty and staff. When they witness areas of misunderstanding, when there is stark disagreement with potential changes, or when there are needs for shifts in direction, frontline leaders adapt and adjust in real time to actualize the agenda and plans. The interactive dimension of planning requires conscious and deliberate attention to who is in the room, what their needs are, and how their responsiveness and adaptation skills will be necessary in revising preactive plans.

Postactive Planning: Reflection and Introspection After Implementation

In addition to planning and designing necessary before and during racial justice work, educators also engage in planning after implementation. This postactive and reflective planning of frontline leaders is an important aspect of the planning process because postactive reflection feeds into the next phase and stages of preactive planning. The planning that occurs after interactive planning and implementation is reflective and might also mostly be done mentally. *Postactive planning* is the planning that happens to inform new and expanded efforts of implementation moving forward. For instance, in the case of a professional development session focused on racial justice, frontline leaders might reflect on the strengths and challenges of the session on their car ride home from the professional learning session. This reflection about the happenings of the session is a form of postactive planning that leaders use to think about future professional learning sessions. Thus, the postactive phase of planning is much like the preactive active phase of planning in that leaders draw from past, similar, analogous experiences to make decisions about the implementation of policies and practices moving forward. Certainly, each of these phases of planning (preactive, interactive, and postactive) relates and connects to the others and they are part of a cyclical process. Figure 3.1 is a visual of the cycle of design and planning described herein.

For frontline leaders, designing and planning must be gauged based on the time and scope of the implementation endeavor. For instance, curriculum mapping or curriculum redesign during the summer months of planning may involve a level of preactive planning (both mentally and written down) that planning for a community partnership event might not. Frontline leaders plan before (preactive), during (interactive), and after (postactive or reflective) they advance racial justice work. To be potentially transformative, this planning must be carefully and deliberately considered. Although so much of the planning of leaders is mentally constructed and occurs at various times of the day, effective frontline leaders view planning and designing racial justice work as essential to the individual and collective success of a classroom, school, and district. These various phases of planning connect and depend on one another.

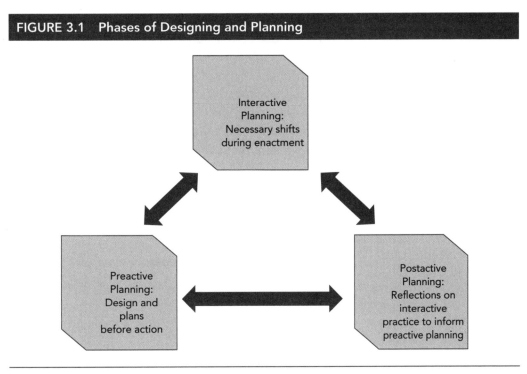

FIGURE 3.1   Phases of Designing and Planning

Source: Jackson (1968).

Planning in Time and Space

Clark and Yinger (1979) found that educators plan at six main levels: yearly, term, unit, weekly, daily, and lesson. These elements of planning are not separate or distinct; rather, they inform and rely on one another for maximized success. Educators' planning at the beginning of the year requires breaking the plans up into terms, the terms into units, the units into weeks, the weeks into daily, and the daily into lessons. Although the writing down of plans has been reported most effective in an informal "grocery list" format (like a "things to do" list or a sketchy outline), primarily to trigger the memory of educators (McCutcheon, 1980), more expansive planning might be necessary during these moments of transience among school leaders, as the knowledge base and awareness of racial justice is new and underdeveloped, and as educators build data repositories in order to improve their knowledge. Clark and Yinger (1988) advise that beginning educators (i.e., those early in their careers) should think of their plans as "flexible frameworks for action, as devices for getting started in the right direction, as something to depart from or elaborate on, rather than as rigid scripts" (p. 13).

Summary and Conclusions

Taken together, school leader and collective leadership should lead to the kinds of designs and planning that bridge and draw from the expertise of a Frontline Leadership collective: centering and learning from the brilliance, voices, and perspective of young people, families, parents, and caregivers, as well as other educators in the school. In short and sum, frontline leaders *search the self* in planning and designing for racial justice. This means that educators search and examine their own current and historical values, beliefs, mindsets, thinking, and beliefs about what is emphasized and executed in schools and classrooms. Searching the self insists that there is synergy between beliefs and worldviews and design practices in schools and classrooms. As they search themselves, frontline leaders *share personal stories of resilience and overcoming* while planning and designing for racial justice. Because young people often see adults (and especially school leaders) as mentors and role models for their own lives, sharing challenges that adults have had can be a site of possibility and motivation for young people.

Some young people may believe, for instance, that adults in schools have never had challenging situations. To the contrary, young people need (and deserve) to know that each of us struggles with succeeding academically and socially throughout our lives. That adults have been able to persevere is an important reminder of how human beings can overcome difficult situations with opportunity centered support structures. Frontline leaders also *partner with and collaborate with families, parents, and caregivers* as they gain a broader community perspective about what is necessary to fight against racism, whiteness, and anti-Black racism. Frontline leaders also *recognize and rely on educator colleagues* to keep them honest about the intricacies of classroom life and the expectations, demands, and realities that propel and stifle the work of racial justice.

Frontline leaders *learn about and with students* while planning and designing for racial justice. This means that school leaders are interacting with young people, talking with them in the corridors, visiting student classes, observing their contributions and insights in classes, inviting them to join committee work in the school, and implementing their interests and expertise in what is designed and carried forward in the school. Related to learning about and with young people, frontline leaders *attend a game, play, concert, or some after-school program of young people* as an aspect of planning and designing for racial justice. Learning from young people is a process that helps school leaders build powerful relationships with them. Showing up at student activities inside and outside of school functions allows school leaders to build solidarity with families and communities and to plan and design related opportunities connected to young people's engagements. Frontline Leadership is steadfast in acknowledging power differentials and constructing spaces where all voices are included in the vision and mission of racial justice.

How to Disrupt Punishment and Pushout Practices

4

Too many school leaders, particularly assistant and associate principals, are forced to fixate on student punishment, masked in the language of school discipline. These school leaders work to maintain order and control over the bodies of young people in a school. They may not realize school leaders should be drawing from and advancing their knowledge and expertise in co-constructing humanizing curriculum and opportunity centered instructional, assessment, and relational practices. Put simply, when school leadership centers humanizing, relevant, and responsive curriculum, instructional, assessment, and relational practices, student behavior challenges tend to decrease (Milner, 2020).

Although we talk about "discipline" and "disciplinary" practices to improve student behavior, what we really are practicing is punishment, as I will be discussing throughout this chapter. These punishment practices are mostly designed to exclude students from a classroom context through school suspension or expulsion. More recently, restorative discipline movements in schools have intensified—without deep knowledge and understanding of the roots, genius, philosophies, and purposes of an alternative approach to suspension, exclusion, and punishment writ large in schools and classrooms. Educators push students out of the classroom to the "restorative discipline" room to work with an educator "trained" in it, and these spaces tend to be just a rebranding of in-school suspension.

Notably, the push for restorative discipline excludes the term *justice* (Winn, 2018) because such an inclusion would require a deep understanding of the ways in which harm and injustice have perpetually pushed young people of color out of the classroom to grim consequences. Taken together, school leadership steeped in a tradition of maintaining law, order, and compliance does not provide leaders opportunities to demonstrate what a school could be; these leaders are not using their knowledge, expertise, insights, and experience to co-plan and co-develop deep, restorative curriculum, instructional, assessment, and relational practices. They are working to ensure lines in the hallways are straight, that students are not talking, that students' shirts are tucked in their pants, and that the leaders have all the control in a space.

In this chapter, I focus on how to disrupt punishment and pushout policies that disproportionately affect students of color. Frontline leaders focus on and cultivate curriculum innovation, instructional connection to the curriculum and student identity, assessment flexibility designed to capture student learning and instructional effectiveness, and healthy relationship enforecement. In particular, frontline leaders tap into their creativity to move beyond business-as-usual mindsets and actions and are committed to supporting their teachers and others in the school to deepen their knowledge, mindsets, beliefs, and understanding of culturally relevant and culturally responsive practices that reduce the need for punishment and pushout practices. Thus, rather than supporting teachers with generic classroom management pre-packaged toolkits, frontline leaders work to support educators in building the kinds of curriculum and instructional practices in schools and classrooms that engage young people, build and honor their racial identities, and help them maximize their potential to participate in a racially just school context. To be sure, when curriculum, instructional, assessment, and relational practices are relevant, responsive, engaged, and steeped in opportunity (as described in Chapter 2), classroom management challenges take care of themselves (Milner et al., 2018). I focus on cultural relevance and responsiveness rather than racial relevance to resist the propensity of educators to follow stereotypes about different racial groups. People in racial groups are not a monolith. There is huge variation among people in and across individuals and communities of color. Culturally relevant and responsive practices take into consideration race, racism, and equitable practices that help frontline leaders maximize curriculum, instructional, assessment, and relational excellence in a school.

Research about school disciplinary and punishment practices is compelling and robust (Davis & Jordan, 1994; Losen, 2011; Skiba et al., 2002; Welsh & Little, 2018). School leaders and other educators—those committed to a profound agenda to lead racially just schools—can and should learn much from this research. For instance, office referrals tend to originate in the classroom, and proportionally teachers refer Black students to the office more often than white students, even for the same offenses (Gregory et al., 2010). Troubling patterns of disproportionality in office referral have been pervasive and consistent over many years. Any school leader concerned about the health of his, her, or their school must understand the historical racist and consistent patterns of punishment and pushout for minoritized students, especially Black students.

Skiba et al. (2002) found a "differential pattern of treatment, originating at the classroom level, wherein [Black] students are referred to the office for infractions that are more subjective in interpretation" (p. 317), whereas white students are referred to the office for infractions that are more "objective." As Losen (2011) explained, for "offenses that require a judgment call by teachers, administrators and others, Black students are disproportionately called out" (p. 7). The disturbing realities for Black students should cause school administrators to understand that while they are responsible for the health, success, outcomes, achievement, and opportunity structures of the entire school, they must intensify their concerns for Black students—given these troubling data points regarding punishment and pushout.

Most office referrals are a result of noncompliance, such as students being out of dress code or not following an arbitrary rule, rather than a threat to safety. Black students are also referred to the office more often than students from other racial groups, even in districts that have a high proportion of Black students (Skiba et al., 1997). In the words of Skiba et al. (1997), "these data provide further evidence of disproportionality in the administration of school discipline based on race" (pp. 313–314). Indeed, Black students continue to experience alarming rates of office referral and suspension. Data from the U.S. Department of Education, Office for Civil Rights (2014), for instance, show that in 2013–2014, Black students represented about 16% of the student population in U.S. public schools but 32% of in-school suspensions and more than 40% of out-of-school suspensions.

Alarmingly, data also show that the disproportionality of Black student office referral, and consequently suspension and expulsion, begins as early as preschool. Data show that although Black students represent 19.5% of preschool enrollment, they made up 48.6% of preschool students suspended once and 53.4% of those suspended more than once (U.S. Department of Education, Office for Civil Rights, 2018). These data would suggest that problems of disproportionate referral, suspension, and expulsion are not improving in preschool.

These exclusionary and punishment practices can result in what educational psychologists call missed "time on task" (Woolfolk, 2019). For instance, Davis and Jordan (1994) explained that exclusionary practices—where students are sent out of the classroom and miss instructional time—can result in Black male student classroom and school "disengagement" (p. 586). It is difficult for Black students, or any group of students, to perform well on standardized examinations or any type of assessment when they are not in the classroom experiencing learning opportunities. Although educators may believe these exclusionary and punishment practices are building discipline among their students, the evidence shows these practices can ultimately harm, not help, Black students. Frontline leaders use these data to help illuminate these trends and patterns, and engage with the Frontline Leadership teams (as discussed and conceptualized in Chapter 3) to address and redress these challenges. To be sure, if not disrupted, punishment and pushout practices will continue to disenfranchise young people of color—and namely Black students as the data consistently show.

Discipline and Punishment Practices

Throughout this book, I have discussed the importance of language precision as a collective endeavor necessary to ensure humanizing, opportunity-rich experiences for all in schools. In this chapter, I challenge frontline leaders to trouble the way the constructs "disciplinary" and "punishment" are used. To be clear, although we refer to office referrals and subsequent suspensions, expulsions, and so forth as "disciplinary practices," the practices are more accurately captured as "punishment practices." In other words, when we exclude young people from school, lower their grades for late work, or take away the phones of young people in school, we are practicing punishment, not necessarily disciplinary practices. While sometimes warranted, punishment may or may not build discipline, if, in fact, discipline is the goal. Thus, I challenge frontline leaders, working in collaboration with their Frontline Leadership communities, to name their practices more appropriately. Are these educators enacting and naming discipline practices or punishment practices? Regardless of the practice, the language of what is being practiced—discipline or punishment—should be more accurately captured. In Table 4.1, I share some differences, as I have conceptualized them, between discipline and punishment practices.

Frontline leaders must be diligent in helping students understand that discipline and punishment are not synonymous (Duncan-Andrade, 2016; Foucault, 1975; Noguera, 2003). My point is not to suggest that discipline and punishment are opposite or mutually exclusive. One practice may be related to and connected to another. For instance, a punishment practice such as removing a student from class for using disrespectful language, if done consistently over time, might lead to a disciplinary practice that eventually shifts the student's "disrespectful" language. Such transformation in this student's talk would likely be dependent on the degree to which the student cares about the subject or the classroom that has pushed the student out for the language offense. Frontline leaders work

TABLE 4.1 Discipline- Versus Punishment-Centered Practices	
DISCIPLINE CENTERED	**PUNISHMENT CENTERED**
Provide multiple opportunities for students to "excel"	Exclude, office refer, suspend, and expel
Focus on cognitively rich and rigorous curriculum and instructional practices	Teach to the test
Communicate and collaborate with families on ways to support student learning and development	Ostracize and marginalize families, parents, and communities
Model tenacity, persistence, and care	Give up on students
Cultivate and envision students as knowledgeable	Act as the arbiter of knowledge and knowing
Invest in the individual to impact the community	Advance an individualistic ethos of success
Build and sustain relationships with students	Create unnecessary distance between students
Engage in real talk about social realities and expectations in society	Engage in surface-level or arbitrary talk or not talk at all
Expand racially centered textual curriculum opportunities	Develop and enact curriculum as white, mainstream, and traditional

to help students build discipline and reject excessive punishment practices that exclude students—large proportions of Black students—from the learning environment.

Noguera (2003) reminded us that disciplinary practices in schools often "bear a striking similarity to the strategies used to punish adults in society" (p. 342). As a tool for discussion and practical application, I am hopeful school leaders will study Table 4.1 and engage with their Frontline Leadership team as well as colleagues to (a) reimagine the language used to describe discipline and punishment practices, (b) foster increased disciplinary practices over punishment practices, and (c) build tools to study the nature of these practices in schools in order to create spaces that are focused on curriculum, instruction, assessment, and relationship practices that can have a significant influence on student learning and development as well as the overall health and vitality of the school community. Shifting punishment practices to those that are discipline centered provides the best chances for young people to succeed because these practices are transferable to their interactions and future situations. It is important to note that much of the insights in the chart related to building discipline practices over punishment practices are related to curriculum, instruction, assessment, and relationship practices that honor and humanize young people in classrooms and schools.

Frontline Leadership focuses on curriculum, instruction, assessment, and relationship practices not only in the classroom but throughout the entire school. *Frontline leaders, who reclaim their rightful space beyond the chief punisher in a school, are keenly focused on curriculum, instruction, assessment, and relationship practices throughout the entire school, as students experience curriculum, pedagogy, assessment, and relationships not only in the classroom but in other spaces as well.* To be clear, I am stressing that school leaders might use Figure 4.1 to help deepen their own and their school's understanding of discipline practices in relation and comparison to punishment practices.

Pressing Toward Discipline

As educators continue to build their curriculum, instruction, assessment, and relationship muscles, they provide multiple opportunities for students to succeed. They do not give up on students, send them out of the classroom, or give them low grades on assignments without designing for them multiple opportunities to learn what has been taught, to adjust their behaviors, and to thrive. In this way, under the leadership and expectations of frontline leaders, educators in a school do not allow students to fail because they view student failure as a failure of the school—the pedagogical, curriculum, assessment, and relational tools in place not designed to respond to and meet the complex opportunity-centered needs of young people. These practices as teachers build them exemplify disciplinary over punishment practices that can have a lasting impact on student learning and development over time.

> Frontline Leadership is committed to cognitively rich and rigorous curriculum and instructional practices, where students are challenged to think deeply, question intently, and apply what they have learned to other social contexts.

Pressing toward discipline over punishment in schools also means that Frontline Leadership is committed to cognitively rich and rigorous curriculum and instructional practices, where students are challenged to think deeply, question intently, and apply what they have learned to other social contexts.

Young people yearn for opportunities to think and push the boundaries of what they believe they know and what is being communicated through curriculum and instructional practices. But this engagement of young people must be done in a non-punitive context because the spaces allow young people to take risks and make mistakes and errors to advance their thinking in potentially profound ways.

Although they may not realize it, young people are observing the behaviors, interactions, temperaments, responses, and perseverance of the adults with whom they work in a school and classroom. Disciplinary practices demand that students not give up on themselves and their potential to improve over time.

Frontline leaders should model the kinds of tenacious and resilient care that they hope their educator colleagues will display. While frontline leaders encourage educators to co-construct spaces where students have multiple opportunities to succeed, they also stress how their embodied interactions and moves demonstrate to young people how young people might respond to similar situations. For instance, frontline leaders make it clear that the school should be a place where adults model tenacity, stick-to-it-iveness, resilience, perseverance, grace, dignity, and integrity in the face of challenges.

> Disciplinary practices demand that students not give up on themselves and their potential to improve over time.

All young people are knowers and experts of their own experiences inside and outside of school. Frontline leaders must cultivate and envision students as knowledgeable and capable of building knowledge and improvement in the school and classrooms. Students sense when adults do not view them as capable, smart, hardworking, insightful, and knowledgeable. To build disciplinary practices, adults must see students as knowers and communicate their belief in their knowledge and capacity to learn and develop in and through explicitly communicative approaches.

Although often following a culture of competition, frontline leaders build school communities where educators invest in the individual students to impact the community. In this way, the school context is seen as a place where community success is valued and honored over individual achievement and success. *Frontline leaders encourage and cultivate collaborative projects among faculty, staff, students, and the broader community to advance disciplinary practices that might improve the human condition.* Indeed, far too many students of color are positioned in competition with white students at an unfair disadvantage. Schools are designed to cater to the worldviews, experiences, preferences, psychological/mental/emotional health, and well-being of white students. When Black and other minoritized students do not conform, change themselves, or assimilate, a culture of competition makes it almost impossible for some Black students to succeed.

Frontline leaders are committed to co-designing experiences where teachers, for instance, build skills to cultivate relationships with young people, families, and communities; engage in *real talk* about the racism, whiteness, and anti-Black racism they experience in schools and society;

and build collective over individual insights about how to amplify and accelerate discipline. Moving away from punishment practices where educators develop and enact curriculum, instructional, assessment, and relationship practices as white, mainstream, and traditional requires schools to examine what practices are common in the school and what practices *should* be. Identifying what more relevant and meaningful disciplinary practices in schools should be requires frontline leaders to study the possibilities from the existing research, through collaboration and contributions with other colleagues within and outside of the school, and from what they come to know and believe about curriculum, instruction, assessment, and relationship practices that are well tied to racial equity and inclusion.

Guided and informed by research on learning and teaching, frontline leaders must support educators as they teach the truth. Building disciplinary practices over punishment practices is a charge that is essential for the health and well-being of not only students but also educators. Educators must be committed to telling the truth. *Especially during times when school boards, politicians, and others are pushing back against curriculum, instruction, assessment, and relationship practices that communicate the truth about race, racism, and anti-Black racism, frontline leaders must demonstrate their unwavering support of educators who are professionals well equipped to teach truth in developmentally appropriate ways.* The work of leadership in the press for truth requires a collective set of discipline among all those in the school. School leaders must be on the frontlines working with colleagues, communities, researchers, theorists, politicians, and others to educate the broader masses about what the research tells us about curriculum, instruction, assessment, and relationship practices that push our country toward a true democracy.

> School leaders must be on the frontlines working with colleagues, communities, researchers, theorists, politicians, and others to educate the broader masses about what the research tells us about curriculum, instruction, assessment, and relationship practices that push our country toward a true democracy.

For instance, we know from the research of Huguley et al. (2019) that student outcomes may improve when students have a strong sense of their own racial identity. This means that educators should develop practices that build students' racial identity and not mute conversations or lie and develop fallacies about American historical and contemporary racialized realities. The work of leadership for truth in the face of undersubstantiated punishment requires that schools build disciplinary practices among all those in the community to persevere and thrive during these uncertain times.

Curriculum Punishment

As discussed throughout previous chapters of this book, the curriculum can be conceptualized as what students have the opportunity to learn in schools (Eisner, 1994; Lee, 2007; McCutcheon, 2002) and outside of schools (Gutiérrez et al., 1999). Students experience curriculum practices through both formal and informal aspects of learning, not just in the classroom. Educators play an enormous role in what gets covered in the curriculum (Banks, 2016; Gay, 2010), and Frontline Leadership must be necessarily strong in supporting the confidence and capacity of teachers and other educators to co-design curriculum practices designed for racial justice. In this sense, educators themselves can be seen as curriculum engineers who co-orchestrate and co-construct, with students, learning opportunities.

I am introducing the concept *curriculum punishment* as a tool to describe how students are harmed when they are not exposed to potentially transformative, racially just learning opportunities in classrooms as schools. Frontline Leadership views curriculum punishment as an essential element of understanding punishment because of racist, anti-Black policies, structures and systems that prevent educators (teachers, coaches, administrators, and school counselors) from exposing students to curriculum and learning opportunities that honor, reflect, and enhance student identity, motivation, interests, and needs. These aspects of curriculum punishment that are taught through the null curriculum (i.e., what is not taught) might include, for example, the Holocaust or Black Wall Street (the Tulsa, Oklahoma, massacre). More than curriculum moves in the classroom, frontline leaders understand that curriculum punishment can (and does) occur throughout the entire community of the school.

The null curriculum—what is not covered—can become a form of curriculum punishment when learning opportunities have the potential to heal, recharge, and transform racially diverse students. It is important to note that curriculum punishment can occur even when educators are not deliberately or intentionally avoiding learning opportunities in a school. *This point—that curriculum punishment can be practiced even when school leaders and other educators are not attempting to avoid, disrupt, or mute the truth about race and racial injustice in schools—is a firm reminder that frontline leaders' mindsets, values, beliefs, and thoughts must be interrogated through self-reflection to recognize what is missing in their own conceptions that can prevent a school culture and community from making racial justice progress. These analytic tools—frameworks that examine what is missing in students' experiences through the null curriculum—translate and carry over into frontline leaders' observations of educators' practices as school leaders are evaluating, correcting, and suggesting practices.*

In sum, curriculum practices are sites of punishment when they are void of potentially transformative learning opportunities for any group of students because of disconnected principals, superintendents, school counselors, teachers, or policymakers. In school communities, who decides what can, cannot, will, or will not be covered in a curriculum? What role will frontline leaders play in ensuring that practices of truth remain central to curriculum, instruction, assessment, and relationships? Further, curriculum punishment happens when Black students are punished for not being white: Black students are expected to assimilate, change themselves, code and culture shift, and negotiate their racial and intersecting identities to deal with and fit into a curriculum, instruction, assessment, and relationship world that results in these students' feelings of disconnectedness, vulnerability, and yearning for a more humanizing learning context. Through anti-Black racism and curriculum punishment, many Black and other minoritized students become drained and frustrated by a school community dedicated to maintaining whiteness. But to be sure, all students are punished for lack of curriculum practices that are racially inclusive and that tell a wide range of truths. Curriculum punishment occurs when the walls in the hallway are bare of Black and indigenous contributions. Curriculum punishment occurs when Black history and announcements about Black people during school announcements only occur during February.

School punishment, a broader conceptual way of thinking about curriculum punishment, is not only a result of material nullification. But because Black school leaders and other educators are texts themselves from which young people can learn, curriculum punishment is also manifest in the declining numbers of Black educators in schools. Black educators may become role models for what and who young people decide they (can) be in schools and society. When young people do not see themselves represented in schools in leadership roles, for example, they experience a form of curriculum punishment based on the lack of embodied Black bodies present in the school.

The *Brown v. Board of Education* (1954) decision resulted in Black teacher and school leader pushout and what has been called a mass exodus of Black educators from U.S. public schools (Foster, 1993; Holmes, 1990; King, 1993; Milner & Howard, 2004). With desegregation came massive layoffs and demotions of Black educators. Schools in the southern districts saw the most dramatic and drastic changes and shifts of Black educators.

Overall, approximately 38,000 Black teachers and administrators lost their positions between 1954 and 1965 in southern states (Holmes, 1990; King, 1993). Research shows that if Black educators were not in fact dismissed, many were demoted or forced to transfer. In the words of Irvine, "They took our best principals and leaders in [the Black] communities and put them into these newly desegregated schools and called them assistant principals. . . . So it was a devastating blow" to Black educators, Black schools, and Black communities (cited in Milner & Howard, 2004). In response to intentional practices of pushing out, reassigning, and demoting Black teachers and school leaders following *Brown*, current research, theory, and practice advance the urgent need of recruiting, retaining, and supporting a more racially diverse cadre of teachers (Ball, 2009; Ball & Tyson, 2011; Cochran-Smith, 1995; Dillard, 2002; Easton-Brooks, 2019; Foster, 1990; King, 1991; Sleeter, 2008; Sleeter & Milner, 2011; Zeichner, 2003).

Irvine and Irvine (2007), in a retrospective analysis of their 1983 examination of the effects of desegregation on the education of Black students, stressed the potential role of educators in perpetuating cycles of office referrals, suspensions, and expulsions, particularly for Black students. Meier et al. (1989), in their study, found that in districts with large numbers of Black teachers, fewer Black students were referred to the office and subsequently suspended or expelled. In this way, Black teachers are not only curriculum texts themselves as well as curriculum engineers where they are working to co-construct racially just contexts, these teachers are also less likely to refer students to the office through a pushout and punishment practice. But the stories of Black principals send the message that they push out and suspend Black students at alarmingly high rates. This means Black school leaders must consider the ways in which they contribute to racial justice.

Since *Brown*, there has been a decline in the Black teaching force while student racial diversity has been intensifying. These declines and reductions in the Black educator force are in contrast to the increasingly diverse racial and ethnic background of students. Research has shown that, particularly before the *Brown* decision, in schools with all-Black students, Black educators understood the social, affective, behavioral, cognitive, intellectual, relational, and academic needs of their students (Foster, 1997; Irvine, 1990; Irvine & Irvine, 1983; Milner & Howard, 2004; Tillman, 2004; Walker, 1996, 2000, 2013). Tillman (2004) reported that Black educators during segregation "saw potential in their Black students, considered them to be intelligent, and were committed to their success" (p. 282). Thus, pushout of not only Black students but also Black educators is also a major concern that school leaders must address as they disrupt curriculum punishment in schools and classrooms across the United States. However, recruiting more Black principals to enact the same or similar oppressive pushout and punishment policies will not move us forward as a nation.

Scripted Curriculum, Instruction, and Assessment as Punishment

As I have written in more depth elsewhere (Milner, 2013), serious conversations are needed about the proliferation of scripted and narrowed curriculum as we work against racism in schools. Districts across the United States continue developing and enforcing policy in which educators are expected to follow scripted curriculum. In addition, the curriculum is narrowing with heavy emphasis on mathematics and language arts to the possible exclusion of other subjects such as music, art, social studies, and physical education. Narrowing of the curriculum refers to the reduction of curriculum content covered to focus in more specifically on subject areas to the decrease or exclusion of other areas. By scripted curriculum, I am referring to a predeveloped set of managed curriculum tools and guidelines that explicitly direct and command educators on what to teach, when to teach it, how to teach what is taught, almost exactly what to say, and how to assess and evaluate learning from the standardized curriculum (Demko, 2010; Ede, 2006; Smagorinsky et al., 2002). The belief is that scripted curriculum, instruction, and assessment practices can ensure that all students are exposed to the same practices regardless of where they live, what they already know and are able to do, their interests, their motivations, their needs, or their propensity to deepen their knowledge in one subject area over another.

Scripted and narrowed curriculum, instruction, and assessment are especially common and pervasive in urban and high-poverty schools, where a central aim is to increase student test score performance (Ede, 2006; Mathis, 2012). In too many instances, teachers teach to standardized forms of measurement and assessments. Notably, students in these schools are typically students of color, students whose first language is not English, and/or students who live below the poverty line. In fact, King and Zucker (2005) maintained that the impetus to narrow the curriculum was shaped in part by the need for teachers to focus on aspects of the curriculum that would be most likely tested in any given year. But what about the knowledge and learning opportunities that students deserve that never show up or are not prioritized on standardized tests? Frontline leaders understand that their work must be more expansive than narrowly focused practices that militarize a learning context in the name of test score lauding. *While my point is that scripted and narrowed curriculum, instruction, and assessment practices can be forms of punishment for all those in a school, I also realize that innovative instructional practices for communities of color, in particular, have not met their needs. My point is certainly not that traditional curriculum, instructional, and assessment practices that fail minoritized communities are any better than scripted, strict, myopic ones. Frontline leaders realize that they must take the best of what is known across contexts of success and achievement and co-construct a community of learning by drawing from what they learn and what is needed to transform their environment.*

Logically, scripted and narrowed curriculum, instruction, and assessment can suggest to the public that educators are automatons rather than professionals solving the complex problems of teaching and learning they encounter. Therefore, frontline leaders must help educate and illuminate the ways in which the public understands and views the intricate nature of educator work. Otherwise, the public might perceive teaching as technical and mindless work, as a profession that does not require them to possess the cognitive ability and professional knowledge, wisdom, and judgment to improve student learning and cultivate student success because curriculum, instructional, and assessment decisions have been predetermined by someone outside of them. In other professions, such as medicine and social work, professionals are expected to be able to learn from the particulars of their working conditions and use their professional knowledge and judgment in responding to strengths and challenges they encounter. Drawing from the best of what we know about practices for success, frontline leaders reject agendas that demand scripted and narrowed curriculum, instructional, and assessment practices that do not honor the wide range of what we know about human development and learning. Because scripted and narrowed curriculum practices seem to only be most appropriate for mostly Black and a few other minoritized communities, frontline leaders are constantly questioning the legitimacy of such practices.

> Frontline leaders realize that they must take the best of what is known across contexts of success and achievement and co-construct a community of learning by drawing from what they learn and what is needed to transform their environment.

Indeed, competing perspectives on the utility, effectiveness, and promise of scripted and narrowed curriculum exist. For instance, one logical argument in support of scripted curriculum points to benefits of a predetermined curriculum for teachers new to the profession of teaching as scripted curriculum, instructional, and assessment materials provide guidance for them in knowing what to teach, when to teach what, and, to a lesser degree, what assessments to use. Moreover, a narrowed, managed, and more focused curriculum with newer teachers may allow them the opportunity to concentrate more succinctly on what students need to know to perform well on high-stakes and other standardized examinations. Although these and other logical arguments exist in support of curriculum scripting and narrowing, teachers are actually punished for their noncompliance with administrative expectations to follow these predeveloped scripts, even though evidence is clear that what is necessary for success in a suburban district might look qualitatively different from what is essential in a rural or urban school (Gay, 2010; Howard, 2010; Irizarry & Donaldson, 2012).

Particularly in schools where resources are scarce, scripted, standardized curricula, instruction, and assessment make it difficult for teachers to understand and respond to the sociological, ecological, and affective composition of the classroom. Especially with populations of students who have been traditionally underserved, Ede (2006) wrote, "the diverse ethnic and cultural makeup of today's classrooms makes it unlikely that one [scripted], single curriculum will meet the needs and interests of all students" (p. 31). Frontline leaders think about the degree to which scripted and narrowed curriculum, instruction, and assessment enables or stifles students' opportunities to learn and develop. Central interrelated questions that frontline leaders might consider include the following: (a) In districts and schools where scripted and narrowed curriculum are the norm, how can teachers be supported to "work through" scripted curriculum to meet the needs of all their students? (b) How can scripted curriculum movements be reorganized to provide agency for teachers regarding how students are taught and how they learn? (c) Beyond examining student test scores, in what ways does scripted curriculum support student learning, and in what ways does it not? As many charter schools are lauded for their success in teaching from a script and fostering drills, chants, and procedures, frontline leaders must examine just what these students are experiencing and why.

Narrowed Curriculum, Instruction, and Assessment as Punishment

In addition to scripted curriculum, instruction, and assessment practices, curriculum narrowing disproportionately influences young people of color and those in high-need schools and districts. Cawelti (2006) pointed out missed learning opportunities for students when teachers focus only on math and language arts/reading at the expense of other subjects. Ede (2006) cautioned against "test-driven" approaches where "rote memorization" takes precedence over critical thinking, creativity, innovation, and other forms of students' expression. Frontline leaders ponder what the short-term and long-term effects of curriculum narrowing might be that prevent students from engaging deeply in social studies, the arts, and physical education, for instance. Banks (2003) maintained that social studies can be a critical subject matter area to shepherd students toward becoming social justice–minded citizens who can solve complicated problems for their communities and beyond. Banks stressed that "the world's greatest problems do not result from people being unable to read and write. They result from people in the world—from different cultures, races, religious and nations—being unable to get along and work together to solve the world's intractable problems" (p. 18).

For sure, high-quality, truth-seeking social studies provides our best chance of creating a more racially just society. Yet, reform efforts are decreasing many students' exposure to social studies. Thus, frontline leaders must grapple with the following questions regarding curriculum narrowing:

1. In what ways does curriculum narrowing de-professionalize and de-skill teaching and teachers, respectively?

2. How might curriculum narrowing interfere with efforts to co-construct robust learning opportunities for young people and adults in a school to work toward racial justice?

3. How do federal and state policies, such as Title I, dictate the kinds of learning opportunities available in schools?

4. How do policies and schools account for the streamlined learning opportunities that students miss via narrowed curriculum designed to increase test scores?

5. How might curriculum narrowing that decreases physical fitness among youth contribute to debilitating diseases such as high blood pressure and high cholesterol among youth?

6. In what ways do the sociopolitical contexts and racial demography of students shape their exposure to narrowed and scripted curriculum?

7. How do policies reconcile potential increases in student test scores in mathematics and language arts with the relatively static or decreased student learning in other academic domains of learning?

Indeed, the overemphasis on reading and math to the exclusion of other subject areas narrows the scope of students' opportunities to learn, and students may suffer if frontline leaders are not drawing from elements of these reform efforts that consider a more holistic picture of student learning and development needs—needs that may never show up on a standardized test such as mental and emotional health, physical fitness, and mindfulness.

But what do educators need to know and be able to do in schools to name, disrupt, counter, and end punishment practices such as scripted and narrowed *curriculum, instruction, and assessment punishment?* Moreover, what do educators need to know to be able to press toward ending racism, whiteness, and anti-Black racism? How do frontline leaders ensure an ethos of learning and development among educators to recognize, acknowledge, and build tools to disrupt injustice while reimagining what happens in schools and classrooms? I explore these knowledge and practice imperatives in the next section of the chapter.

What Educators Need to Know and Be Able to Do

Ladson-Billings (2006) shared the following regarding a representative interaction she had with a prospective teacher. The prospective teacher expressed the following concern to Ladson-Billings: "Everybody keeps telling us about multicultural education, but nobody is telling us how to do it!" (p. 30). Perplexing to many of those in her audience, Ladson-Billings's response was, "Even if we could tell you how to do it, I would not want us to tell you how to do it" (p. 39). For Ladson-Billings, there were at least two important lessons inherent to her response to the teacher who queried about how to "do" multicultural education and essentially equity work. For one, educators work with a range of students who bring enormously robust dimensions of diversity into learning environments. Although frontline leaders will be knowledgeable and support a transformative learning context, there is no one-size-fits-all approach to the work of teaching and certainly none for racial justice work. Educators must be mindful of whom they are teaching and the range of needs that students bring into the classroom. Moreover, the social context that shapes students' experiences is vast and complexly integral to what decisions are made, how decisions are made, and with whom. The nature of students' needs will surely vary from year to year, from classroom to classroom, and from school to school. *In this way, what educators should do in the work of racial justice, I am stressing, is aligned with what they know and how they think.* Thus, Frontline Leadership is committed to helping educators develop the mind and heart for racial justice work—more than demanding a set of predetermined, prepackaged practices.

A second point to Ladson-Billings's (2006) response to the teacher who complained that she was not being told how to "do" multicultural education is that no one tells us how to "do democracy" (p. 39); we just do it. I would suggest that we as a nation do not necessarily "do" multicultural education as much as we pursue it. In a similar light, educators who practice culturally relevant practices do so because it is consistent with what they believe, how they think, and who they are. Frontline leaders stress the notion that educators' conceptions guide their practices based on their knowledge and understandings of contextual realities that can be transformative in the lives of young people.

Shulman (1987) pointed to the necessity of teachers' development of subject matter knowledge as well as pedagogical knowledge. He stressed the convergence of the two: teachers' pedagogical content knowledge (i.e., the knowledge teachers have of their content) and how they teach that content to their students. Clearly, teachers' knowledge about and ability to teach their subject is necessary for student success in any classroom. However, some school leaders, other educators, policymakers, and community-school advocates believe subject matter expertise is the only real important feature to student and teacher success. I have observed that these leaders might admit there are other aspects of teacher learning and development that are essential, but many believe that subject matter knowledge is all that *really* matters in and through classroom instruction. Knowledge and expertise in a subject area does not necessarily mean educators will know and understand the content they are teaching through racialized lenses. Moreover, knowledge of subject matter and pedagogy are deeply connected to teachers' knowledge about assessment that should be guided by their relationships with students. Such convergence of knowledge and knowing—the interconnectedness of curriculum, instruction, assessment, and relationships—allows teachers to make necessary adjustments in the classroom for student learning.

On a broader scale, alternative, fast-track teacher training programs such as Teach for America (TFA) recruit noneducation majors into teaching under a premise that their corps members have content knowledge, having earned an undergraduate degree in a particular domain such as history or mathematics. Frontline Leadership then requires the posing of critical questions about what knowledge is, how knowledge is constructed and validated, and who decides the worth, value, and meanings of knowledge (Apple, 2006) among educators. In other words, frontline leaders have to decide whether subject matter knowledge is sufficient for the kinds of curriculum, instructional, assessment, and relational practices necessary to promote racial justice and equity in schools. When teachers do not have certification through traditional teacher education programs, it is frontline leaders' responsibility to support these teachers in building the kinds of knowledge necessary for student success.

Certainly, I agree teachers must have deep, rich, and nuanced subject matter expertise to facilitate learning opportunities in a classroom. However, I recall experiences as a student in high school and college when it was clear teachers possessed a wide and deep range of knowledge in their subject domain but were not strong instructors of that content.

Their assessments were dry and mundane—mostly relying on scantrons and multiple-choice questions. These educators had very poor relationships with their students. They delivered direct instruction and did not increase my interest or deep engagement in the subject area.

While some teachers were able to draw from their subject expertise and convey it effectively to students, others did not have the ability to teach and assess the subjects well. As a student in college, I recall several higher-level mathematics and history professors who knew their subjects well—they were well-respected experts in their respective fields of research—but struggled to deeply illuminate complex mathematical ideas or historical moments and movements, or investigate why students in their classes were successful or not. Indeed, frontline leaders must understand that just because a teacher has a deep-level subject matter knowledge does not necessarily mean he, she, or they can or will be successful teaching for racial justice.

As curriculum and instructional leaders pressing toward racial justice, frontline leaders must co-construct environments where teachers and other educators in their schools build the knowledge, attitudes, ideas, ideals, dispositions, mindsets, frameworks, beliefs, values, and practices that propel them to (1) build powerful and sustainable relationships with young people; (2) view, plan, and design classroom management strategies and skills through an emphasis on restorative justice, curriculum, instruction, assessment, and relationship practices; (3) learn more about the historical context and landscape of a community and school; (4) engage and participate in the sociopolitical landscape of the school in which they work; (5) co-develop partnerships with family members of their students, the community, and other stakeholders; (6) work collaboratively with their colleagues and other school leaders for student success; (7) build appropriate, humanizing, and meaningful assessment tools; (8) learn about and build on and from interests of students and the community; (9) identify, recognize, and build on assets of all students, the community, and their colleagues; (10) reflect, recognize, and understand their own strengths and cultivate them; (11) visualize their work as a developmental process and commit themselves to growing and developing to meet and exceed the complex needs of their students; (12) contextualize, transform, and translate standards in ways that are instructionally innovative, curricular connected, relationally sustaining, and assessment rich; (13) develop anti-racist practices such as culturally relevant instructional practices, culturally responsive instructional materials, opportunity centered practices, engaged pedagogical practices, and restorative justice practices.

Although much research has been done about educators' subject matter knowledge and their pedagogical knowledge and skills, frontline leaders must simultaneously cultivate racial knowledge among educators.

Racial Knowledge

Elsewhere I have described the racial knowledge teachers need (Milner, 2003) and enact in preK–12 classrooms (Howard & Milner, 2021) with students to address structural and systemic punishment practices I described previously in this chapter. However, educators' building knowledge about race is insufficient in the grand narrative of what it takes to transform schools into spaces of racial justice and equity. As Shulman stressed in his conceptualization of teachers' subject matter knowledge, I stress educators need to be equipped to practice racial justice throughout the school day and across different social contexts.

It is important to note that teachers work within organizational structures and systems that can either propel their knowledge or hinder it. Building racial knowledge requires that educators attempt to understand aspects of themselves more deeply, others, structures, systems, mechanisms, and practices that perpetuate and/or maintain the status quo. The research supports the idea that when teachers develop the disposition to continue building their racial knowledge, they can be difference-makers for their students in classrooms because their racial knowledge helps them advocate for their students inside and outside of the classroom (Milner, 2020). Building racial knowledge requires teachers to rethink what they thought they understood previously; at times, educators may be frustrated by the knowledge-deepening process. But they understand that racial knowledge construction is lifelong work that can elevate over time. Frontline leaders stress and advance racial knowledge, opportunities, and expectations by doing the following:

- Understanding that racial knowledge and knowing is interdependent on and in communion with others.

- Studying the rich, complex, and nuanced *history* of race and the people of color educators serve.

- Problematizing, critiquing, and questioning white norms, white privilege, white fragility, white manipulations, and white supremacy.

- Examining how equity, not solely equality, can improve the educational experiences of all students and especially students of color. Good examples for educators to build their knowledge include funding formulas in districts where per pupil spending in schools varies significantly and correlates with race across the United States.

- Interrogating how punitive disciplinary policy and practices such as in-school suspension, out-of-school suspension, and expulsion can do more harm than good for students. Educators deepen their knowledge by considering how outcomes are impacted when students miss important instructional opportunities because they have been pushed out of classrooms and schools.

- Investigating alternative practices such as restorative justice to resolve conflicts and help students and educators heal and work together for emancipatory experiences. Rather than adopting a predetermined set of practices that educators attempt to implement without deep introspection, care, and conviction in schools, the idea is that educators instead study aspects of promising practices and transfer the features that are most relevant, responsive, and opportunity centered to their particular circumstance.

- Listening to families and communities of color who have mostly been silent. Families and communities are the experts of their experiences and when educators listen to their personal and collective stories, they are better able to deepen their racial knowledge and serve students.

- Identifying and building on the many assets and strengths of students and communities of color.

- Developing and enacting curriculum, instructional, assessment, and relational practices that explicitly align with assets of students and communities of color.

- Recognizing and building insights about how to explicitly disrupt racial inequity and injustice. In other words, racial knowledge requires educators to be in the trenches advocating for equity on behalf of their students even when they believe they have little control over the policies that have been developed. In this way, educators understand the ways in which systems and structures work to disenfranchise, harm, demoralize, and traumatize communities of color.

Conceptualized together, the twelve interrelated practices I discussed in the previous section relate to supporting educators in centering curriculum, instruction, assessment, and relational practices. Focusing on these four areas (curriculum, instruction, assessment, and relationships) allows frontline leaders to shift away from punishment and pushout so that all students might experience schooling spaces they desire.

Although several of the practices described next are framed through the lens of culture, grounded in research, practice, and praxis, I bring the practices forward as tools to assist frontline leaders in the work of co-creating a professional learning ethos of racial justice in schools because each of the research practices centers explicit attention on race, whiteness, anti-Black racism, as well as other forms of racialized oppression. Rather than advancing the idea that frontline leaders should build culturally responsive practices themselves, my point is that these leaders must know what culturally relevant and culturally responsive practices are and look like for the educators with whom they work—mostly teachers who interact with young people for hours each day.

> Focusing on these four areas (curriculum, instruction, assessment, and relationships) allows frontline leaders to shift away from punishment and pushout so that all students might experience schooling spaces they desire.

Culturally Relevant Practices

Researchers have made a compelling case for the importance of educators developing culturally relevant curriculum, instruction, assessment, and relational practices with students, all students, in preK–12 classrooms (Howard, 2001; Ladson-Billings, 1994; Milner, 2016). Ladson-Billings (1992), the scholar responsible for conceptualizing culturally relevant pedagogy, maintained that it is an approach that "uses the students' culture to help them create meaning and understand the world. Thus, not only academic success, but also social and cultural success is emphasized" (p. 110).

The construct suggests that students develop a critical consciousness and that they move beyond spaces where they simply or solely consume knowledge without critically examining it and its relation to their own experiences, identity, aspirations, and needs. Although this approach is framed mostly as pedagogical practice, frontline leaders can learn much from this research about teaching to attempt to cultivate it across school. For sure, frontline leaders need to know when they see and observe racially just practices, to acknowledge and celebrate them, and hopefully to provide spaces where other educators in the school can draw and learn from such practices.

The point is that teachers create learning environments where student voices and perspectives are amplified and students are allowed to participate (more fully) in the multiple discourses available in a learning context by not only consuming information but also helping to deconstruct and to construct it (Freire, 1998) in relevant ways for their lives and learning. Explaining the importance of voice and experience through what she called "engaged pedagogy," hooks (1994) wrote,

> As a teacher, I recognize that students from marginalized groups enter classrooms within institutions where their voices have been neither heard nor welcomed, whether these students discuss facts—those that any of us might know—or personal experience. My pedagogy has been shaped to respond to this reality. If I do not wish to see these students use the "authority of experience" as a means of asserting voice, I can circumvent this possible misuse of power by bringing to the classroom pedagogical strategies that affirm their presence, their right to speak, in multiple ways on diverse topics. (p. 84)

Thus, frontline leaders assume that all students bring to the classroom knowledge that is experiential, knowledge that matters, and knowledge that is substantiated based on the students' experience and expertise. Ladson-Billings (1994) further explained that culturally relevant pedagogy

> uses student culture in order to maintain it and to transcend the negative effects of the dominant culture. The negative effects are brought about, for example, by not seeing one's history, culture, or background represented in the textbook or curriculum. . . . Culturally relevant teaching is a pedagogy that empowers students intellectually, socially, emotionally, and politically by using cultural referents to impart knowledge, skills, and attitudes. (pp. 17–18)

Educators who co-create culturally relevant learning contexts are those who see students' culture as an asset, not a detriment, to their success. Teachers use student cultural practices in curriculum planning and design, instructional innovation and implementation, assessment agility, and relational connectedness.

Young people develop skills and dispositions to question how power struc-tures are created and maintained in U.S. society. Students are expected to develop intellectually and socially to build skills that make meaningful and transformative contributions to society. Culturally relevant pedagogy is an approach that helps students "see the contradictions and inequi-ties" (Ladson-Billings, 1992, p. 382) that exist inside and outside of the classroom. Building a culturally relevant school environment means that frontline leaders shepherd educators (and young people) into spaces of inquiry about racial inequity and to fight against the many -*isms* and pho-bias that they encounter while insisting that students build knowledge to transfer and apply to other experiences. In essence, frontline leaders push, advocate for, design, build collectives with, and advance school contexts that are *questioning spaces* and spaces *in search of truth*—where all are probing about the health of a school and community. To be sure, Frontline Leadership must be guided by the answers to carefully constructed ques-tions that help us learn and know more to get better.

Frontline leaders advance culturally relevant practices because they believe in them, and they come to know that culturally relevant practices foster, support, create, and enable racial justice practices that do not reify stereotypes but rather honor the dynamic role race plays in culture. Thus, race is an essential dimension of culture and cultural practices. People are not told how to do democracy because democratic principles are infiltrated throughout U.S. society. Ladson-Billings suggested that people practice democracy because they believe in a fundamental value of what it means to live in the United States. More than a set of principles, ideas, or predetermined practices, culturally relevant practices emanate from a state of being or mindset that permeates school environments. How do school leaders organize, rally with, and design spaces where people adopt a mindset and conceptual framework for culturally relevant contexts?

Culturally relevant pedagogy is *relationally grounded*. Frontline leaders co-create space where all students feel valued, validated, cared about, and cared for. Adults perceive students' race as a resource and not a lia-bility to enhance learning opportunities and relationships. Relationships with young people necessitate spaces where young people's voices and perspectives are normalized. These spaces afford students opportunities to think about what is happening in their local communities and to com-plete projects that address matters they can understand locally. Although many educators claim to support practices of cultural relevance, very few are able to articulate what they know about the features and tenets of culturally relevant pedagogy.

Tenets of Culturally Relevant Pedagogy

I have been stunned by the number of school leaders and other educators who employ culturally relevant and/or culturally responsive language but do not know what the tenets and major features of the practices are. As frontline leaders who are well informed and whose practices are guided by research, knowing, and explaining, modeling and embodying practices help educators build a sense of confidence and faith in their leader and also in their own capacity to practice cultural relevance. Three interrelated tenets shape Ladson-Billings's conception of culturally relevant pedagogy: academic achievement, sociopolitical consciousness, and cultural competence. When "pedagogy" is used, Ladson-Billings is referring to the theory. When "teaching" is used, Ladson-Billings is referring to the practice of the theory.

Ladson-Billings (2006) expressed her regret for using the term *academic achievement* when she first conceptualized the theory, partly because educators immediately equated academic achievement with student test scores. What Ladson-Billings (2006) envisioned was that culturally relevant pedagogy would allow for and facilitate student learning: "what it is that students actually know and are able to do as a result of pedagogical interactions with skilled teachers" (p. 34). Academic achievement, then, is about student learning. Frontline leaders do not see student learning as tied only to a classroom. Rather, frontline leaders see their role of cultivating academic achievement through relevance and relatability throughout the entire school community. For sure, frontline leaders support teachers in building practices for student learning. But the school context should be seen as a canvas with carefully and deliberately designed learning opportunities for students pushing for racial equity and justice.

> They see their role of cultivating academic achievement through relevance and relatability throughout the entire school community.

A second tenet of culturally relevant pedagogy, according to Ladson-Billings, is sociopolitical consciousness. Sociopolitical consciousness is about the micro- (school and district), meso- (community and state), and macro- (nation and world) level matters that have a bearing on educators and students' lived experiences and educational interactions. For instance, the idea that unemployment, poverty, and inflation rates influence national debates as well as local community needs is a sociopolitical matter that may relevantly, developmentally, and appropriately inform curriculum, instruction, and assessment opportunities that shape social consciousness. Sociopolitical consciousness is not about *frontline leaders and other educators pushing their own political and social agendas.* Sociopolitical consciousness is about helping "students use the various skills they learn to better understand and critique their social position and context" (Ladson-Billings, 2006, p. 37) and to hopefully do something to improve human experience through social action about injustice.

The third tenet of culturally relevant pedagogy for Ladson-Billings is cultural competence. Cultural competence is not necessarily about helping educators develop a set of static insights about differing cultural and racial groups to develop some sensitivity toward another culture or cultural practices they do not know. Rather, for Ladson-Billings, cultural competence is about student acquisition of cultural knowledge regarding their own cultural ways and systems of knowing society. Such a position, Ladson-Billings explained, with a focus on the pursuit of cultural competence being focused on students, runs counter to how other disciplines such as medicine, nursing, clergy, and social work may think about and conceptualize cultural competence.

In medicine, for instance, physicians are sometimes trained to develop a set of knowledge about differing cultural groups to complement their ability to work with people who may be very different from them. For instance, it seems viable and quite logical for younger physicians to be educated to work with older patients. Bedside manner for physicians might also be enhanced when they develop knowledge about people living in poverty or people from a different racial or ethnic background from theirs. The notion that physicians are attempting to deepen their knowledge base about cultural groups for which they have very little knowledge and understanding can serve as essential learning for physicians if they realize the enormous range of diversity inherent within and among various cultural groups of people and as they realize how and why culture and cultural practices shift among people. Where race is concerned, people sometimes misuse the term *culture* by collapsing all individuals in a particular race together.

> Where race is concerned, people sometimes misuse the term *culture* by collapsing all individuals in a particular race together.

The term *African American* denotes an ethnic group of people, not a singular, static cultural group. There is a wide range of diversity among and between African Americans although there are some consistencies as well. African Americans share a history of slavery, Jim Crow, and other forms of systemic discrimination and racism that bind the group. At the same time, African Americans possess a shared history of spiritual grounding, tenacity, and resilience through some of the most horrific situations that human beings have had to endure. However, while there are shared experiences, there are also many differences between and among African Americans. A risk of such training, where physicians acquire knowledge about varying cultural groups toward cultural competence, is reification of stereotypes.

Thus, what Ladson-Billings means by cultural competence is "helping students to recognize and honor their own cultural beliefs and practices while acquiring access to wider culture, where they are likely to have a chance at improving their . . . status and making informed decisions about the lives they wish to lead" (p. 36). In culturally relevant practices, school leaders push cultural competence to help foster student learning about themselves, others, and how the world works to be able to function effectively in it, transform it, and contribute to it. Indeed, frontline leaders know and understand that people from different races enter schools where those in the environment co-construct culture and cultural practices together.

Potential Outcomes of Culturally Relevant Practices

But what are connections between culturally relevant practices and student outcomes? That is, what are potential student outcomes when frontline leaders lead by advancing an ethos of culturally relevant practices? The answer to this question is not one that, I believe, can be answered by looking exclusively at students' test score performance. Rather, the outcomes of culturally relevant practices extend far beyond what might be measured on a standardized exam. Grounded in Ladson-Billings's ideology, as well as my own research, student outcomes can be captured in at least three broad categories—especially if readers are willing to think of student outcomes to be prevalent and possible beyond traditional test score measures.

One outcome is the amplification of student voice. In too many schools with large populations of students of color, students are expected to suppress their voices and perspectives. As an outcome, students are encouraged to examine intently what they are learning, to create and to construct meaning, to contribute to the multiple conversations in a classroom with agency, to succeed academically and socially, and to gauge contradictions and inequities both in school and outside of school. In addition, culturally relevant practices insist that students see their culture (and race!) in curriculum, instruction, and assessment practices. Young people are encouraged to maintain and sustain their own racial identity and not suppress it. Student voices intensify when students feel connected to the curriculum and the school. Seeing themselves in the curriculum and through instruction and assessment helps students understand the important ways in which their lived embodied experiences contribute to various genres of curriculum content and to the fabric of U.S. and broader society. And a third outcome is students learn about the social and political realities of the micro, meso, and macro and consciously work to solve and contribute to ending racism, whiteness, and anti-Black racism. As frontline leaders endeavor to disrupt and press toward ending racism, whiteness, and anti-Black racism, culturally relevant practices center on the curriculum, instruction, assessment, and relational practices.

Culturally Responsive Teaching

As is the case with culturally relevant practices, many school leaders are unable to define, conceptualize, or articulate tenets of culturally responsive practices even though they may claim such aspirational practices for their school. Frontline leaders must insist that educators study their students (Ladson-Billings, 2009) and use students' experiences as cultural data sets (Lee, 2007) to maximize students' opportunities to learn. Studying students means that educators are not blind to the racism that students experience throughout their daily and otherwise experiences. Scholar Geneva Gay conceptualized culturally responsive teaching as

> using cultural knowledge, prior experiences, frames of reference, and performance styles of ethnically diverse students to make learning encounters more relevant to and effective for them. It teaches to and through the strengths of these students. . . . [It] is the behavioral expressions of knowledge, beliefs, and values that recognize the importance of racial and cultural diversity in learning. (p. 31)

Culturally responsive teaching situates race as central, not tangential, to the teaching and learning exchange (Howard, 2010; Irvine, 2003; Milner, 2020).

In framing the principles of culturally responsive practices, Gay outlined several conventions: (1) culture [and race] counts—the idea that culture and race should be viewed as an asset and complementary to the educational process is essential; (2) conventional reform is inadequate—Gay maintained that current efforts to reform and transform schools have been underwhelming in terms of improvements for some of our most vulnerable students in schools; (3) intention without action is insufficient—there is a strong practice and implementation aspect to the ways in which Gay frames culturally responsive practices; (4) strength and vitality of cultural and racial diversity—the idea is that there is important value in racial diversity: "diversity is a strength—a persistent, vitalizing force in our personal and civic lives" (Gay, 2010, p. 15); and (5) test scores and grades are symptoms, not causes, of achievement problems—centralizing the reality that culturally responsive practices pose the kinds of questions that address under(Lie)ing reasons for challenges students face and not look at test scores and grades as the only, nor the main, data point in understanding and responding to student challenges (Milner, 2012).

Tenets of Culturally Responsive Pedagogy

As educators are building knowledge about, sharpening, and/or advancing their capacity to be curriculum, instructional, assessment, and relational leaders, they must study and be able to articulate what research shows about practices of culturally responsive teaching that lead to racial justice and racial equity. I focus on six tenets or principles that shape culturally responsive practices, according to Gay:

- *Culturally responsive practices are validating.* These practices affirm, sustain, and acknowledge cultural and racial backgrounds, experiences, worldviews, ideas, ideals, and values of students and their families. Validation also means that educators understand and merge outside-of-school realities with those inside of school and work *with,* not against, student preferences and interests.

- *Culturally responsive practices are comprehensive.* This practice takes a holistic view—similar to the ways in which hooks (1994) explained engagement (as discussed earlier in this chapter). Educators understand and attempt to build on and respond to students' "social, emotional, and political learning" (Gay, 2010, p. 32) in making decisions about what should and should not happen in a school. The idea here is that it is difficult to maximize student learning opportunities and engagement when we are not attentive to the wide range of students' humanity—such as their mental, emotional, and psychological health.

- *Culturally responsive practices are multidimensional.* Educators understand that their work must be designed and redirected to address multiple modalities of student learning and development. As a site to deepen their knowledge about historical and contemporary issues of race, whiteness, and anti-Black racism, frontline leaders encourage and co-create learning opportunities in school with young people and educators to hear from community members and nontraditional educators and watch documentaries, movies, and other learning tools together moving beyond traditional, stale, and mundane practices. Frontline leaders embrace the idea that "curriculum content, learning context, classroom climate, student-teacher relationships, instructional techniques, classroom management, and performance assessments" (Gay,

2010, p. 33) are interrelated and must be considered throughout the entire school through diverse and varied modes.

- *Culturally responsive practices are empowering.* Young people already have power, and educators should reject the notion that they must grant empowerment and control of the hearts, minds, and spirits of young people. Instead, school leaders must cultivate spaces where young people recognize their own power and freedom of expression to bring the fullness of themselves to a learning environment.

- *Culturally responsive practices are transformative.* Frontline Leadership supports and encourages those in the school to examine, know more about, make curriculum connections to, and make contributions to the community. As change agents working toward racial transformation, frontline leaders engage and create an ethos where young people are building sophisticated, nuanced, and complex knowledge about community to improve it. This transformative work requires that we recognize strengths of a community while concurrently identifying challenges in order to change them. For example, students are taught to "analyze the effects of inequities on different ethnic individuals and groups, have zero tolerance for these, and become change agents committed to promoting greater equality, justice, and power balances" (Gay, 2010, p. 37).

- *Culturally responsive practices are emancipatory.* This stance of Frontline Leadership presses toward a liberatory process where educators recognize the power of education and learning beyond satisfying predetermined sets of requirements in a classroom or school. In other words, students develop an emancipatory worldview of their experiences that rejects too much schooling (Shujaa, 1998) in favor of education. Indeed, schooling and education are not synonymous; students come to understand that it is difficult to press toward freedom for or with others until one is liberated himself, herself, or themself (West, 1993). Freedom is an outcome of education, not schooling.

Summary and Conclusions

To conclude, when I was in graduate school, my grandmother (who was not formally educated and lived to the age of 92 years old) would often ask me about the work I was doing. Excited to share, I would often talk about the demanding challenges I faced with my work, particularly concerning racial justice. I talked about nonsensical policies that seemed to perpetuate and maintain the status quo. I would tell her about funding challenges that seemed to further marginalize communities of color. I would share how frustrating it was that high school students were working part-time jobs to support their families and still expected to "produce" the same outputs as those who did not have to work. I talked about how inequitable, unfair, unjust, and alarming situations were (and are) in society and education. One day after I finished my analyses and critiques about education, schooling, and society, my grandmother looked at me, paused, frowned a bit at me, and said, "Well, keep pressing, baby!"

I suspect these words may feel under-nuanced or perhaps even unthinkable during these times of uncertainty. For sure, for frontline leaders attempting to recruit new teachers who are committed to racial justice, retain current ones who are unafraid of political backlash against the truth, cultivate and support young people to maintain their racial identity and maximize their potential, and partner with families, parents, and communities, the work is far from easy or simple. But what I have presented in this chapter should provide an intense space of framing for frontline leaders who understand that the work of equity, while difficult, must continue to be pursued because truth, democracy, public education, teacher professionalism, and racial justice are all on the line. We have made significant progress toward racial justice and equity over the years, and I employ frontline leaders and other educators to remember that our young people, families, communities, policymakers, and colleagues need them unlike ever before. So, let's *keep pressing*!

> We have made significant progress toward racial justice and equity over the years, and I employ frontline leaders and other educators to remember that our young people, families, communities, policymakers, and fellow colleagues need them unlike ever before.

No Turning Back

Conclusions, Summaries, Recommendations, and Implications

5

In this book, I have advanced Frontline Leadership as a necessary imperative stance, mindset, and set of emergent, iterative, responsive, opportunity-centered, and humanizing practices as we fight against racism and for truth in schools throughout the United States. More than a set of static practices, Frontline Leadership requires school leaders to build their intellectual, research, mindset, and advocacy muscles to co-construct contexts where young people and educators thrive. So, Frontline Leadership is about how leaders think about their work as they build practice. Building from the many lessons I have learned from my own research and that of others over the years from teachers, young people, families, parents, community members, policymakers, educational advocates, and leaders, I shed light on what leaders and leadership must do *now*. By specifying the time is *now*, I focus on the urgency of the moment in which educators and young people find themselves. I focus also on the intricate and complex challenges educators are facing as their professional judgment is being called into question on many different fronts. In addition, I center the current social and political moment as a necessary imperative to consider in the work of justice and equity.

Frontline Leadership moves beyond stale, dated, predetermined, irrelevant, under-responsive, disconnected, and "racially neutral" decision making with an explicit focus on building policy and practices that move us closer to racial justice and equity. Frontline Leadership disrupts and moves beyond a white-centric framework to how the world works and how the world should work in education. Frontline Leadership is an approach to co-constructing an ethos of healing, hope, possibility, and transformation where school leaders aggressively, deliberately, and persistently work to end punishment and pushout practices and co-build curricula, instructional, assessment, and relational health in their schools.

Frontline Leadership is not well conceptualized in educational leadership studies. Much of what I found in the established literature regarding Frontline Leadership was from the fields of medicine, nursing, and industry. Across this literature were several important themes. Chief among the literature on Frontline Leadership was the insight that Frontline leaders build both clinical expertise as well as organizational leadership knowledge, expertise, and skills to succeed. Moreover, Frontline Leadership was mostly conceptualized as a practice of up-front, rather than behind-the-scenes, practices, where workers and professionals motivate, direct, guide, articulate, support, and develop others in making effective decisions. Frontline Leadership also builds the capacity to understand, respond to, and cultivate truth-telling cultures during what is characterized as uncertain and complex times.

Moving away from the idea that school leadership should be inundated with maintaining order and controlling the bodies, minds, joy, spirits, actions, desires, and hearts of young people and others, Frontline Leadership is concerned with leaders who center and build capacity for outstanding curriculum, instructional, assessment, and relational practices. In fact, throughout this book, I focus on these four interconnected areas because, as I have studied the effectiveness of practices and practitioners in education, these four dimensions are drivers of success in schools of racial justice and equity.

Throughout this book, I highlight and provide explicit examples of what Frontline leaders and Frontline Leadership must entail. Frontline leaders (a) work to close opportunity gaps and disrupt racism, whiteness, and anti-Black racism; (b) co-develop systematic plans and designs to combat and confront racial injustice in schools; and (c) stop punishment and pushout practices to amplify the curriculum, instructional, and relational health of schools.

Although the previous chapters are inundated with specific strategies emerging from my own research and that of the broader research community, some readers will still muse that they do not know what to do to advance racial justice in their schools. Some might even claim that they do not know how to build the mindsets, beliefs, attitudes, and dispositions necessary for this complex and ever-changing work. I conclude this book with several additional recommendations in addition to some concluding thoughts about the enormously important work ahead for frontline leaders and all educators. To be sure, I realize schools and consequently educators cannot solve all our challenges of racism, whiteness, and anti-Black racism. Frontline leaders are resolute, however, in their commitment to work on addressing those issues as part of the collective aims for justice. Although racial justice work needs to be carried forward carefully, astutely, grounded in research and practice, centering young voices and engagement, the work is urgent, and the work must happen now.

In the next section of this conclusion, I provide brief profiles of school leaders doing the work of racial justice. Some advance racial justice work more keenly and dedicated than do others. Frontline leaders are invited to think about what aspects of their beliefs, dispositions, and practices show up in the profiles that follow.

Profiles of Problematic Leadership Stances and Practices

In this section, I pull together elements of *problematic stances* and practices of school leaders I have observed, talked with, heard, read about, or witnessed as an educational researcher, parent, and educational advocate.

Frontline leaders insist that schools move away from the following stances: (a) *Race and color avoidance stances*—where educators stay away from the ugly roots, contemporary lies, and racist, anti-Black practices of curriculum, instruction, assessment, and relationships connected to race in schools. (b) *"Everybody matters" stances.* Some believe that the Black Lives Matter movement excludes other groups of people; these people profess that "everybody matters." Frontline leaders stress that it is difficult to articulate or believe that everybody matters when too many Black lives do not. (c) *"They will figure it out" stances.* Some educators follow an approach to race talk, race work, and other racialized issues that suggests that "life" will teach young people how to navigate race, racism, whiteness, and anti-Black racism. Frontline leaders stress that the work of educators is to do race work and to help young people be well-prepared for the issues they (will) face. (d) *"Someone else will teach them" stances.* Even when they realize young people are thinking about race, reinforcing racial hierarchies, and/or experiencing racism and racial subordination, some educators may believe it is someone else's job and responsibility in the school (or outside of it) to address these issues.

In addition to these stances, I name and conceptualize problematic practices of school leaders' work related to racial justice as Hiders, Talkers, Theorists, Obstructors, Stallers, Pleasers, Sporadic Doers, and External Motivators. More than a set of individual traits, the snapshots of these groups of leaders are better considered as ways to think about, articulate, and name problematic pracitices when observed. In other words, if we see Frontline Leadership or the leadership of any educator as a trait of an individual, we misunderstand the reality that people practice and move forward agendas. Critiques and transferable features should be examined based on the behaviors of enactors, not the people themselves. For instance, the issues we face with whiteness are those related to what is practiced, executed, and enacted in schools and the broader social world, not to white people, per se. To be clear, reflect on all the Black principals reifying whiteness in schools every single day. In short, whiteness, in fact, can be practiced through the bodies of a range of people, including people of color.

Hiders

Some school leaders sit in the background and hide in the fight against racism. They find ways to not be seen during conversations about truth, whiteness, and white supremacy. They believe they can be apolitical, see their role and responsibility as a school leader as strictly a job, and hide from and are evasive or elusive in the quest to build policies and practices that address racism, whiteness, and anti-Black racism. These school leaders sit in the back during district, state, and conference convenings and other professional learning opportunities where they are being challenged to show commitment and/or voice a real position against racial justice and injustice. These school leaders hide, believing that they can just sail through thirty years of service and retire. Hiders are dangerous because their nonchalant, noncommittal, docile, and otherwise apathetic dispositions do little to transform their schools toward spaces where all children succeed.

Talkers

Other school leaders are Talkers and not doers. They sit up front in meetings, take up lots of discourse space during professional development, and learn all the latest buzzwords and jargon about racial justice. Although talk is a powerful political move toward action, these Talkers are more concerned about sounding committed to racial justice than planning and designing opportunities for substantive, long-term, scalable, and transformative changes. Talkers are those school leaders who talk more than they listen, who talk more than they read, and who care more about being accepted by a "woke" crowd than moving the talk into equity action. Talkers turn off doers because they derail action with their longwinded positions on issues.

Theorists

Related to Talkers are Theorists. Whether written or orally, these school leaders communicate ideas to others about racial (in)equity in the most complex ways. These school leaders use new, underknown acronyms, constructs, recommendations, and methodologies in communicating with others. Such school leaders have a difficult time moving theory into action or conceptualizing theories of action and change through how they communicate. Because educators may not understand "high theory," school leaders may lose the communication power of the ideas of the theory because they lack the capacity to translate the theory into practice and very little movement happens toward racial justice.

Obstructors

Some school leaders strategically find reasons to stall, hinder, and otherwise block racial justice and equity progress. These leaders look for policies and guidelines to undermine progress their leadership team and other colleagues recommend for more inclusive, racially just contexts. These leaders find any reason possible to ostracize educators committed to racial justice. They are critical of justice-minded colleagues, make their teaching and other workloads stressful and heavier, look over these people for promotions, and marginalize justice-centered colleagues within the school community.

Stallers

Some school leaders believe their primary role is to make sure racial justice moves at the moderately slow rate that white people will be able to accept. These school leaders disguise slow progress forward with fear, inability, and lack of desire and motivation to move forward. These school leaders are *progress killers*, hoping that their delaying will cause people in the community to forget, move away from, tire away from, or redirect efforts away from racial justice and equity. Stallers are like but different from Obstructors. Stallers do not try to hinder racial justice progress as much as they try to prolong it. While Stallers and Obstructors are often working in the background to ensure no real structural and systemic efforts are actualized with respect to racial equity, Obstructors are deliberately working to prevent progress.

Pleasers

Some school leaders believe they can only make racial justice decisions if everybody agrees or when all members of their community are participatory. These school leaders operate from a position that they must have full buy-in before transforming communities to disrupt racism, whiteness, and anti-Black racism. Worried that someone or groups of people may not approve or like their decisions (or them), Pleasers avoid racial justice efforts such as professional learning and development for staff, racially just curriculum and instructional mapping, equity audits, or community meetings. These school leaders care more about their political standings and being accepted and embraced by whiteness than doing what is right for young people and communities of color.

Sporadic Doers

Other school leaders are doers but are not guided by principled, valued, long-term, and research outcomes. They are consistently busy and rarely take time to read, co-plan and co-design, talk with others, study the social context, or even rest and recharge. Their actions are not well linked and aligned. These school leaders rarely respond to emails. They operate from a position of urgency without careful frameworks and theories of change to guide them. Always putting out fires related to racial justice, Sporadic Doers are disorganized and haphazard in advancing racial justice work and initiatives. Doers may believe they are making an impact in the school but may not understand how their sporadic, disorganized practices and behaviors do little to make meaningful racial justice impacts. They gain little trust from others because these school leaders are seen as unreflective and scattered in vision and mission related to how communities should conceptualize and enact racial justice work.

External Motivators

These school leaders believe their chief role is to drive, stimulate, and inspire those in their community to engage fully in the work of racial justice. External Motivators reward faculty, staff, students, families, parents, and community members for working to make the school community more inclusive, but most of their motivating efforts are a function of work outside of themselves. Rarely do these leaders model or embody the practices that they stimulate. These leaders see the work of racial justice as work that others may and should do but embrace very few of the Frontline practices described in this book themselves.

Rarely are the practices described in Table 5.1 singularly enacted. More times than not, elements of these stances or practices emerge across leaders at different times. However, these practices can make moving the work of racial justice daunting, frustrating, and nearly impossible to accomplish and achieve. These are the very practices that I am hopeful frontline leaders contemplate as they build their own knowledge and create spaces of racial justice. Next, I provide some recommendations frontline leaders might consider in building school communities of opportunity—those where every single young person is hopeful and optimistic finds refuge and peace, and is well connected to the people, projects, initiatives, curriculum, instruction, and assessment practices.

TABLE 5.1   Profiles of Problematic Leadership Practices

PROBLEMATIC LEADERSHIP STANCES AND PRACTICES	LEADERSHIP MOVES
Hiders	Some school leaders sit in the background and hide in the fight against racism. They find ways to not be seen during conversations about truth, whiteness, and white supremacy.
Talkers	Some school leaders are talkers and not doers. They sit up front in meetings, take up lots of discourse space during professional development, and learn all the latest buzzwords and jargon about racial justice.
Theorists	Whether written or orally, some school leaders communicate ideas to others about racial (in)equity in the most inaccessible and complex ways.
Obstructors	Some school leaders strategically find reasons to hinder and otherwise block racial justice and progress.
Stallers	Some school leaders are *progress killers*, hoping that their delaying will cause people in the community to forget, move away from, or redirect efforts to achieve racial justice and equity.
Pleasers	Some school leaders believe they can only make racial justice decisions if everybody agrees or when all members of their community are participatory.
Sporadic Doers	Some school leaders are consistently busy and rarely take time to read, co-plan and co-design, talk with others, study the social context, or even rest and recharge. Their doing is disconnected and disaligned across initiatives with little real significant progress.
External Motivators	Some school leaders attempt to inspire outside of themselves. Rarely do these leaders model or embody the practices that they stimulate.

Recommendations for Collective Deliberation for Action

Racial Justice Theme for the Year. Frontline Leadership visualizes what they hope to accomplish in a school—designing and planning at yearly, term/semester, monthly, weekly, and daily intervals (a point that is stressed in greater detail in Chapter 3). Frontline leaders might develop a theme for the academic year directly linked to racial justice. This theme is co-developed with the Frontline Leadership team community and should run parallel with programming, curriculum engineering, innovative instruction, flexible assessment, and community-driven relationship opportunities that allow school personnel to build thematic synergy with young people, families, parents, and communities.

Racial Justice Community Book Reading. Related to the collective school-wide theme, frontline leaders might identify one schoolwide reading where all in the community are engaged with the book. Of course, the book must be developmentally appropriate, and the community book reading is much more seamlessly accomplished with high school students and families. In all cases, adults should engage in the reading that students are reading, and in relevant and appropriate cases young people will be able to read professional development and professional learning texts intended for educator audiences. To be clear, I am hopeful that some young people will adopt this book and read it along with the adults in the school. This reading of young people allows them to critique, explore, nuance, agree with, push back against, and contemplate their own schooling experiences and ways to improve them. A community-wide book reading could be well connected to the theme of the year, and the Frontline Leadership team would be actively involved in selecting the theme of the year along with the community book selection.

Community Racial Autobiography. Johnson (2002) wrote about the power of the racial autobiography in working to prepare educators for the enormous range of racial diversity they would encounter in schools and classrooms. I have adapted the experience and employed this practice of a racial autobiography with my own students along with engaging in the practice myself as a facilitator and teacher educator. The Frontline Leadership team of the school should engage in and support the entire faculty and staff in reflecting about and writing their own racial autobiographies. These racial autobiographies are important because they guide and shepherd educators into thinking deeply about what they teach, how they teach, what they employ as assessments and how they assess, and the essence of their relationships with young people and others. Perhaps more important than the end product of writing a racial autobiography is the process of constructing it. The racial autobiography experience allows educators to understand much about their work. Understanding pivotal moments in one's life helps educators understand their values, belief systems, worldviews, insecurities, power, and privilege in and through situations.

I have found in my own research that the process and product of the racial autobiography can have lasting impacts on teachers' practices and leaders' leadership. They query how their own raced worldviews, perspectives, and insights have been formed. In other words, white teachers who have gone to school with and lived around mostly white people their entire lives are guided in a process to think about how their histories impact their present views and practices with others, communities in which they have had very few interactions outside of reading about others, watching reports of them on the local news, or observing other people in a sporting event or in the shopping mall.

In addition to powerfully guided reflection about race, racism, whiteness, and anti-Black racism, educators draft a written racial identity development/awareness document, describing their memories and thoughts about how they came/have come to see themselves as a racial being. On a small scale, educators pose questions to their parents, teachers, siblings, and friends about events, episodes, and *moments* that shaped how they see themselves as a racial being. Mostly, educators rely on their own memories, thoughts, and reflections about how they came to understand, represent, and develop their racial awareness. After writing the racial autobiography, educators share aspects of it with their colleagues if they feel comfortable sharing. It should be noted that many assumptions about people and why they think, believe, and act the way they do might be more deeply understood through the racial autobiography.

The informal oral sharing of some of the racial autobiography might focus on various "stages" of personal racial identity development and/or on different themes that inform one's racial identity development. Educators are encouraged to share artifacts that complement their story (photos and other memorabilia/documents) to humanize the experience. Guiding questions that may shape the written and oral racial autobiography for all those in a school include, but certainly are not limited to, the following:

1. When (what moments come to mind) did I start seeing myself as a racial being? Where was I, what happened, who was there, and why?

2. What current and historical experiences (in particular) have helped shape my racial awareness?

3. What moments in my family, school, and community shaped my views about race, racism, and other forms of discrimination?

4. What artifacts help tell my racialized story?

5. How might my experiences as a racial being affect me as an educator, affect my current work, and affect my future work in the designing of racially just curriculum, instructional, assessment, and relational practices?

6. What has changed, if anything, about how I see race, racism, anti-Black racism, and other forms of discrimination over the years, and why?

7. What do I hope to change about how I see race, racism, whiteness, anti-Black racism, and other forms of discrimination in my work

as a leader, educator, community member, family member, and/or parent?

The Frontline Leadership team should model this practice and invite their colleagues to be vulnerable in a courageous environment designed to help educators become more effective in the fight for racial justice. Indeed, this process can help people work toward healing the damage caused by racialized hate, stereotypes, misunderstandings, and unawareness. It is important to note that reflecting on, writing about, and sharing such profound memories can elicit traumatizing, hurtful, and challenging reflections.

Frontline leaders and Frontline Leadership teams must decide the degree to which they and their colleagues are prepared for this important introspective work that can have positive, effective implications for their work to help improve the lived experiences of the communities of color with whom they are working. Professional knowledge and judgment are essential for this recommendation to have the kind of influence that it could and should have. For instance, I have observed many fears among educators who engage in this work. Whether fears result in resurrected trauma or high emotional trauma, Frontline Leadership considers the potential benefits and challenges of this exercise. In sum, the racial autobiography provides a triad experience—reflection, writing, and sharing—that is, vocalizing aspects of the story with colleagues in the school. If the infrastructure allows, these autobiographies might live online and be revised each year as new experiences emerge.

When the school community is at a developmentally, socially, psychologically, emotionally, and cognitively appropriate level, young people should be involved in racial autobiographical work *along with* faculty, staff, and leadership in a school. To be sure, many schools at different grade levels encourage students to reflect about, write, and speak about some form of their family history. What tends to be missing are themes related to race. The racial autobiography insists that race is not rejected in this triad of reflecting, writing, and talking about the self. Regardless, it will be essential to learn from young people about how they are doing (a point that was expounded upon in Chapter 3). Along with the expansive discussion about student involvement in Frontline Leadership discussed in Chapter 3, *a young people's listening series* allows educators to learn from and draw on the brilliance of the young people with whom they are working. More than anything, we must listen to the experiences of young people, particularly Black, Brown, and other racialized students who experience schools that are not well aligned with what is necessary for them to experience the fullness of education.

Encourage the Amplification of Story. Related to constructing racial autobiographies is the recommendation to amplify stories within a school community. Frontline leaders understand that we all have stories from which we live and can grow and develop. Amplifying stories across discipline and place is an excellent opportunity to build human connections between and among each other in a school, even when surface-level divisions such as skin color and phenotype are manifest. Frontline leaders stress to all those in an environment that we have stories about our experiences in our science and math classes in addition to the many narratives we come to reflect on and share with our families and communities about our interests, challenges, inspirations, and needs.

Amplifying stories pushes the reflecting, writing, and speaking triad to spaces where the community can talk about their fear and anxieties related to math or their psychological struggles with drafting extensive papers in language arts class. The point is for frontline leaders to cultivate students' interest in storying and re-narrating because of the potential benefit of reflecting, connecting, and learning about, from, and with each other. Storying allows us to (a) consistently and persistently learn about ourselves and others beyond the surface and the mundane; (b) emphasize the richness and possibility embedded in human connections that we might not know, believe, recognize, or understand otherwise; and (c) invite others to think about their own stories related to racial diversity and how those narratives have shaped who they are and what they believe (thus far) about themselves, others, and what they do.

Elevate the Morning Meeting (PreK–12). Frontline Leadership models and cultivates schoolwide and classroom-level opportunities for young people and educators to connect and to build community connections to communicate what is happening with them both outside and inside of the school building, every day of a school year. I am recommending that the "morning meeting" is incorporated prekindergarten through grade 12 to allow students and educators the opportunity to "check in" with students, humanize the learning space, and assist educators in learning more about students to inform their practices (curriculum, instructional, assessment, and relational). So, the morning meeting should be viewed as more than an opportunity for young people to feel connected.

The morning meeting can be a powerful opportunity for educators to learn from their planning and design work of racial justice and equity.

The morning meeting in classrooms prioritizes student voice, and leadership teams should be equipped to support educators in cultivating the kinds of spaces that allow students and educators to talk together through schoolwide meetings as well as classroom meetings. When appropriate, frontline leaders join the meetings of classroom communities too, so that they can learn about ways to build the broader curriculum, instructional, assessment, and relational practices necessary for broader community success. In short, although the morning meeting movement has been most pervasive in elementary schools, I am suggesting that the morning meeting be a permanent part of the life of schools across the grade span.

Several summative reminders and recommendations for frontline leaders and other educators are italicized in this paragraph. These interrelated recommendations are especially for educators during a time when education and educators are experiencing deep de-professionalization, public backlash, and a lack of faith and trust. I am hopeful that school leaders will *remember their why of the work*. Remembering why they are in the profession can be a source of inspiration and persistence even during challenging times. *Share the why and realities of the work*. Rather than sitting on the sidelines and allowing falsehoods and lies to perpetuate, educators should educate others about why they teach. *Build data points and counterpoints*. School leaders have built rich and robust repositories of "data" that show the influence and power of their work. They should share these data with local and broader communities. *Work closely with families, parents, and communities*. Families, parents, and communities know their children well and can come to know their schools well. Build collective efforts designed to work together for shared insight. *Build resource repositories*. Work across communities (educators, community members, policymakers, and especially young people) to build toolkits that respond to efforts of/for racial inequity. *Amplify student voice.* The most powerful data point for resilience and reminders of the why of the work we do should come from the insights of young people. Work with and rely on young people to express themselves about the many restorative and transformative experiences they have had with educators in schools.

Conclusions

There is no question that U.S. society is becoming increasingly diverse. This diversity spans race, ethnicity, socioeconomic status, gender, sexual orientation, geography, educational background, ability (cognitive, social, physical), religion, health, and language. Increasing students' capacity to live within a democracy will be a critical component to our vitality as a nation-state. We will not all agree on the solutions to every issue, and because issues of race, racism, whiteness, and anti-Black racism are so polarizing, our charge is even more difficult. However, although we may not all agree on solutions forward, we should all agree that we aspire to live in a democracy where a collective identity of civility, kindness, empathy, care, and human dignity should prevail and traverse any form of hate we have toward each other as individuals or groups of people.

If schools do not help us get race right, society will regress to times even unparalleled to some of the most horrific times in history, such as slavery and the Holocaust. I am aware that, as curriculum theorist Gordon (1990) expressed, it is difficult for a group of people or an individual to critique and work to change the world when the world works for that group of people or for that individual. Clearly, the need to focus on racial justice in schools is not limited to a sociological community argument related to how people treat each other. To the contrary—the need to center racial justice in the work we do in schools must keenly and unapologetically focus on curriculum, instruction, assessment, and relationships. The infusion of racial justice and equity are charges that frontline leaders embrace. The time is now. We cannot wait. We need Frontline Leadership in the fight against racism in America's schools as we press toward truth.

References

Chapter 1

Alridge, D. P. (2003). The dilemmas, challenges, and duality of an African-American educational historian. *Educational Researcher, 32*(9), 25–34.

Alvarez, A. (2017). "Seeing their eyes in the rearview mirror": Identifying and responding to students' challenging experiences. *Equity & Excellence in Education, 50*(1), 53–67.

Alvarez, A., & Milner, H. R. (2018). Exploring teachers' beliefs and feelings about race and police violence. *Teaching Education, 29*(4), 383–394.

Anderson, J. D. (1988). *The education of Blacks in the South, 1860–1935.* University of North Carolina Press.

Annamma, S. A. (2014). Disabling juvenile justice: Engaging the stories of incarcerated young women of color with disabilities. *Remedial and Special Education, 35*(5), 313–324.

Beatty, D., & Leyva, L. A. (2016). A framework for understanding whiteness in mathematics education. *Journal of Urban Mathematics Education, 9*(2), 49–80.

Bell, D. A. (1980). *Brown v. Board of Education* and the interest-convergence dilemma. *Harvard Law Review, 93*(3), 518–533.

Bell, D. A. (2004). *Silent covenants:* Brown v. Board of Education *and the unfulfilled hopes for racial reform.* Oxford University Press.

Bennett, J. S., Driver, M. K., & Trent, S. C. (2019). Real or ideal? A narrative literature review addressing white

privilege in teacher education. *Urban Education, 54*(7), 891–918. https://doi .org/10.1177/0042085917690205

Berman, G., & Paradies, Y. (2010). Racism, disadvantage and multi-culturalism: Towards effective anti-racist praxis. *Ethnic and Racial Studies, 33*(2), 214–232.

Block, L. A. M., & Manning, L. J. (2007). A systemic approach to developing frontline leaders in healthcare. *Leadership in Health Services, 20*(2), 85–96.

Boutte, G. S. (2016). *Educating African American students: And how are the children?* Routledge.

Bunning, R. L. (2000). Ensuring effectiveness in our front-line leaders. *Industrial and Commercial Training, 32*(3), 99–105.

Cabrera, N. L., Watson, J. S., & Franklin, J. D. (2016). Racial arrested development: A critical whiteness analysis of the campus ecology. *Journal of College Student Development, 57*(2), 119–134.

Carter, R. T. (2007). Racism and psychological and emotional injury: Recognizing and assessing race-based traumatic stress. *Counseling Psychologist, 35*(1), 13–105.

Castagno, A. E. (2013). Multicultural education and the protection of whiteness. *American Journal of Education, 120*(1), 101–128.

Castagno, A. E., & Lee, S. J. (2007). Native mascots and ethnic fraud in higher education: Using tribal critical race theory and the interest convergence principle as an analytic tool. *Equity and Excellence in Education, 40*, 3–13.

Cherry, N. L. (2014). The frontline: A new focus for learning about leadership. *Australian*

Journal of Emergency Management, 29(2), 31–34.

Diamond, J. B., Posey-Maddox, L., & Velazquez, M. (2021). Reframing suburbs: Race, place and opportunity in suburban educational spaces. *Educational Researcher, 50*(4), 249–255.

Dumas, M. J. (2016). Against the dark: Antiblackness in education policy and discourse. *Theory Into Practice, 55*(1), 11–19.

Evans-Winters, V. E., & Hines, D. E. (2020). Unmasking white fragility: How whiteness and white student resistance impacts anti-racist education. *Whiteness and Education, 5*(1), 1–16.

Farinde-Wu, A. (2018). #Blackwomenatwork: Teaching and retention in urban schools. *Urban Review, 50*(2), 247–266.

Fergus, E. (2017). "Because I'm light skin . . . they think I'm Italian": Mexican students' experiences of racialization in predominantly white schools. *Urban Education, 52*(4), 460–490.

Ford, D. Y. (2021). *Recruiting and retaining culturally different students in gifted education.* Routledge.

Fylkesnes, S. (2018). Whiteness in teacher education research discourses: A review of the use and meaning making of the term *cultural diversity. Teaching and Teacher Education, 71*, 24–33.

Goldring, E., & Sims, P. (2005). Modeling creative and courageous school leadership through district-community-university partnerships. *Educational Policy, 19*(1), 223–249.

Gooden, M. A., & O'Doherty, A. (2014). Do you see what I see? Fostering aspiring leaders' racial awareness. *Urban Education, 50*(2), 225–255.

Green, T. L. (2015). Places of inequality, places of possibility: Mapping "opportunity in geography" across urban school-communities. *Urban Review, 47*(4), 717–741.

Harper, S., & Donnor, J. K. (Eds.). (2017). *Scandals in college sports.* Routledge.

Harris, C. I. (1993). Whiteness as property. *Harvard Law Review, 106*(8), 1707–1791.

Jeavons, R. (2011). Developing leadership skills at the front line. *Nursing Management, 18*(6), 24–25.

Kohli, R. (2021). *Teachers of color: Resisting racism and reclaiming education.* Harvard Education Press.

Ladson-Billings, G. (1999). Preparing teachers for diverse student populations: A critical race theory perspective. *Review of Research in Education, 24*, 211–247.

Ladson-Billings, G., & Tate, B. (1995). Toward a critical race theory of education. *Teachers College Record, 97*(1), 47–67.

Laughter, J. (2018). Race in *Educational Researcher:* A technical comment on Li and Koedel. *Educational Researcher, 47*(4), 259–261.

Lee, Y., Douglass, A., Zeng, S., Wiehe Lopes, A., & Reyes, A. (2022). Preparing early educators as frontline leaders and change agents with a leadership development initiative. *International Journal of Child Care and Education Policy, 16*(1), 1–18.

Leonardo, Z., & Manning, L. (2017). White historical activity theory: Toward a critical understanding of white zones of proximal development. *Race Ethnicity and Education, 20*(1), 15–29.

Liu, L., & McMurray, A. J. (2004). Frontline leaders: The entry point for leadership development in the manufacturing industry. *Journal of European Industrial Training, 28*(2/3/4), 339–352.

Lopez, G. R. (2003). The (racially neutral) politics of education: A critical race theory perspective. *Educational Administration Quarterly, 39*(1), 68–94.

Lynn, M., & Dixson, A. (Eds.). (2022). *The handbook of critical race theory in education* (2nd ed.). Routledge.

McGee, E. O. (2021). *Black, brown, bruised: How racialized STEM education stifles innovation.* Harvard Education Press.

McGee, E., Alvarez, A. J., & Milner, H. R. (2016). Colorism as a salient space of race in the preparation of teachers. *Theory Into Practice, 55*(1), 69–79.

Milner, H. R. (2015). *Rac(e)ing to class: Confronting poverty and race in schools and classrooms.* Harvard Education Press.

Milner, H. R. (2020a). Black teacher: White school. *Theory Into Practice, 59*(4), 400–408.

Milner, H. R. (2020b). *Start where you are but don't stay there: Understanding diversity, opportunity gaps, and teaching in today's classrooms* (2nd ed.). Harvard Education Press.

Milner, H. R., & Howard, T. C. (2013). Counter-narrative as method: Race, policy and research for teacher education. *Race, Ethnicity and Education, 16*(4), 536–561.

Milner, H. R., & Lomotey, K. (2014). *Handbook of urban education*. Routledge.

Monroe, C. R. (2013). Coloring educational research: African American life and schooling as an exemplar. *Educational Researcher, 42*, 9–19.

Morris, M. (2016). *Pushout: The criminalization of Black girls in schools*. The New Press.

Morris, J. E., & Monroe, C. R. (2009). Why study the U.S. South? The nexus of race and place in investigating Black student achievement. *Educational Researcher, 38*, 21–36.

Muhammad, G. (2023). *Unearthing joy: A guide to culturally and historically responsive teaching and learning*. Scholastic.

Noordegraaf, M., Schneider, M. M. E., Van Rensen, E. L. J., & Boselie, J. P. P. E. F. (2016). Cultural complementarity: Reshaping professional and organizational logics in developing frontline medical leadership. *Public Management Review, 18*(8), 1111–1137.

Ohnmacht, S. D. (2012). The value of developing frontline leaders in health care. *Journal of Psychological Issues in Organizational Culture, 3*(1), 61–69.

Pearman, F. A. (2020). Gentrification, geography, and the declining enrollment of neighborhood schools. *Urban Education, 55*(2), 183–215.

Ross, S. N. (2013). The politics of politeness: Theorizing race, gender, and education in white southern space. *Counterpoints, 412*, 143–159.

Sealey-Ruiz, Y. (2016). Why Black girls' literacies matter: New literacies for a new era. *English Education, 48*(4), 290–298.

Singer, J. N. (2016). African American male college athletes' narratives on education and racism. *Urban Education, 51*(9), 1065–1095.

Sleeter, C. E. (2017). Critical race theory and the whiteness of teacher education. *Urban Education, 52*(2), 155–169.

Tanner, S. J. (2019). Whiteness is a white problem: Whiteness in English education. *English Education, 51*(2), 182–199.

Tate, W. F. (2008). "Geography of opportunity": Poverty, place, and educational outcomes. *Educational Researcher, 37*(7), 397–411.

Tatum, B. D. (2001). Professional development: An important partner in antiracist teacher education. In S. H. King & L. A. Castenell (Eds.), *Racism and racial inequality: Implications for teacher education* (pp. 51–58). AACTE Publications.

Walker, V. S. (1996). *Their highest potential: An African American school community in the segregated South*. University of North Carolina Press.

Williams, S. M. (2018). African American education in rural communities in the deep South: "Making the impossible possible." In M. McShane & A. Smarick (Eds.), *No longer forgotten: The triumphs and struggles of rural education in America* (pp. 29–44). Rowman & Littlefield.

Chapter 2

Bandura, A. (1986). *Social foundations of thought and action: A social cognitive theory*. Prentice Hall.

Bandura, A. (1996). *Self-efficacy in changing societies*. Cambridge University Press.

Banks, J. A. (1998). Curriculum transformation. In J. A. Banks (Ed.), *An introduction to multicultural education* (2nd ed., pp. 21–34). Allyn & Bacon.

Cornfield, D. B., & Fletcher, B. (1998). Institutional constraints on social movement "frame extension": Shifts in the legislative agenda of the American federation of labor, 1881–1955. *Social Forces, 76*(4), 1305–1321.

Delpit, L. (1995). *Other people's children: Cultural conflict in the classroom*. New Press.

Duncan-Andrade, J., & Morrell, E. (2005). Turn up that radio teacher: Popular cultural pedagogy in new century urban schools. *Journal of School Leadership, 15*, 284–308.

Gay, G. (2010). *Culturally responsive teaching: Theory, research, and practice*. Teachers College Press.

Freire, P. (1998). *Pedagogy of the oppressed.* Continuum.

Haberman, M. (2000). Urban schools: Day camps or custodial centers? *Phi Delta Kappan, 82*(3), 203–208.

Howard, T. C. (2010). *Why race and culture matter: Closing the achievement gap in American classrooms.* Teachers College Press.

Irvine, J. J. (2010). Foreword. In H. R. Milner (Ed.), *Culture, curriculum, and identity in education* (pp. xi–xv). Palgrave Macmillan.

Ladson-Billings, G. (2006). From the achievement gap to the education debt: Understanding achievement in U.S. schools. *Educational Researcher, 35*(7), 3–12. https://ed618.pbworks.com/f/From%20 Achievement%20Gap%20to%20 Education%20Debt.pdf*

Ladson-Billings, G. (2009). *The dreamkeepers: Successful teachers of African-American children.* Jossey-Bass.

Love, B. (2019). *We want to do more than survive: Abolitionist teaching and the pursuit of educational freedom.* Beacon Press.

Milner, H. R. (2008). Disrupting deficit notions of difference: Counter-narratives of teachers and community in urban education. *Teaching and Teacher Education, 24*(6), 1573–1598.

Milner, H. R. (2020a). *Brown* lecture: Disrupting punitive practices and policies: Rac(e)ing back to teaching, teacher preparation, and *Brown. Educational Researcher, 49*(3), 147–160.

Milner, H. R. (2020b). Disrupting racism and whiteness in researching a "science" of reading. *Reading Research Quarterly, 55,* 249–253.

Milner, H. R. (2020c). *Start where you are but don't stay there: Understanding diversity, opportunity gaps, and teaching in today's classrooms* (2nd ed.). Harvard Education Press.

Milner, H. R., & Howard, T. C. (2013). Counter-narrative as method: Race, policy and research for teacher education. *Race, Ethnicity and Education, 16*(4), 536–561.

Morris, A. D. (1984). *The origins of the civil rights movement: Black communities organizing for change.* Free Press.

World Health Organization. (n.d.). *Health and well-being.* https://www.who.int/data/gho/ data/major-themes/health-and-well-being

Chapter 3

Clark, C. M., & Yinger, R. J. (1979). Teachers' thinking. In P. L. Peterson & H. J. Walberg (Eds.), *Research on teaching* (pp. 231–263). McCutchan.

Clark, C. M., & Yinger, R. (1988). Teacher planning. In D. Berliner & B. Rosenshine (Eds.), *Talks to teachers* (pp. 342–365). Random House.

Delpit, L. (1995). *Other people's children: Cultural conflict in the classroom.* New Press.

Dillard, C. B. (2000). The substance of things hoped for, the evidence of things not seen: Examining an endarkened feminist epistemology in educational research and leadership. *International Journal of Qualitative Studies in Education, 13*(6), 661–681.

Doyle, W. (1983). Academic work. *Review of Educational Research, 53*(2), 159–199.

Freire, P. (1998). *Pedagogy of the oppressed.* Continuum.

hooks, b. (1994). *Teaching to transgress: Education as the practice of freedom.* Routledge.

Jackson, P. (1968). *Life in classrooms.* Teachers College Press.

Ladson-Billings, G., & Tate, W. F. (1995). Toward a critical race theory of education. *Teachers College Record, 97*(1), 47–68.

Marks, H. M. (2000). Student engagement in instructional activity: Patterns in the elementary, middle, and high school years. *American Educational Research Journal, 37*(1), 153–184.

McCutcheon, G. (1980). How do elementary school teachers plan? The nature of planning and influences on it. *Elementary School Journal, 8,* 14–23.

Milner, H. R. (2007). Race, culture, and researcher positionality: Working through dangers seen, unseen, and unforeseen. *Educational Researcher, 36*(7), 388–400.

Milner, H. R. (2020). *Start where you are, but don't stay there: Understanding diversity, opportunity gaps, and teaching in today's classrooms* (2nd ed.). Harvard Education Press.

Milner, H. R., Cunningham, H. B., Delale-O'Connor, L., & Kestenberg, E. G. (2018). *"These kids are out of control": Why we must reimagine "classroom management" for equity.* Corwin.

Newmann, F. M., Wehlage, G. G., & Lamborn, S. D. (1992). The significance and sources of student engagement. In F. M. Newmann (Ed.), *Student engagement and achievement in American secondary schools* (pp. 11–39). Teachers College Press.

Tillman, L. C. (2002). Culturally sensitive research approaches: An African-American perspective. *Educational Researcher, 31*(9), 3–12.

West, C. (1993). *Race matters.* Beacon Press.

Woolfolk, A. E. (1998). *Readings in educational psychology.* Prentice Hall/Allyn & Bacon.

Chapter 4

Apple, M. W. (2006). *Educating the "right" way: Markets, standards, God, and inequality.* Routledge.

Ball, A. F. (2009). Toward a theory of generative change in culturally and linguistically complex classrooms. *American Educational Research Journal, 46*(1), 45–72.

Ball, A. F., & Tyson, C. A. (Eds.). (2011). *Studying diversity in teacher education.* Rowman & Littlefield.

Banks, J. A. (2003). Teaching literacy for social justice and global citizenship. *Language Arts, 81*(1), 18–19.

Banks, J. A. (2016). *Cultural diversity and education: Foundations, curriculum, and teaching.* Routledge.

Brown v. Board of Education, 347 U.S. 483 (1954).

Cawelti, G. (2006). The side effects of NCLB. *Educational Leadership, 64*(3), 64–68.

Cochran-Smith, M. (1995). Uncertain allies: Understanding the boundaries of race and teaching. *Harvard Educational Review, 65*(4), 541–571.

Davis, J. E., & Jordan, W. J. (1994). The effects of school context, structure, and experiences on African American males in middle and high school. *Journal of Negro Education, 63*(4), 570–587.

Demko, M. (2010). Teachers become zombies: The ugly side of scripted reading curriculum. *Voices From the Middle, 17*(3), 62–64.

Dillard, C. B. (2002). Walking ourselves back home: The education of teachers with/in the world. *Journal of Teacher Education, 53*(5), 383–392.

Duncan-Andrade, J. (2016). Rose in the concrete. In M. L.-S. Levy (Ed.), *Children from the other America* (pp. 83–95). Brill.

Easton-Brooks, D. (2019). *Ethnic matching: Academic success of students of color.* Rowman & Littlefield.

Ede, A. (2006). Scripted curriculum: Is it a prescription for success? *Childhood Education, 83*(1), 29–32.

Eisner, E. W. (1994). *The educational imagination: On the design and evaluation of school programs.* Macmillan.

Foster, M. (1990). The politics of race: Through the eyes of African-American teachers. *Journal of Education, 172*(3), 123–141.

Foster, M. (1993). Othermothers: Exploring the educational philosophy of Black American woman teachers. In M. Arnot & K. Weiler (Eds.), *Feminism and social justice in education: International perspectives* (pp. 101–123). Falmer Press.

Foster, M. (1997). *Black teachers on teaching.* New Press.

Foucault, M. (1975). *Discipline and punish: The birth of the prison.* Vintage Books.

Freire, P. (1998). *Pedagogy of the oppressed.* Continuum.

Gay, G. (2010). *Culturally responsive teaching: Theory, research, and practice* (2nd ed.). Teachers College Press.

Gregory, A., Cornell, D., Fan, X., Sheras, P., Shih, T. H., & Huang, F. (2010). Authoritative school discipline: High school practices associated with lower bullying and victimization. *Journal of Educational Psychology, 102*(2), 483–496.

Gutiérrez, K. D., Baquedano-López, P., & Tejeda, C. (1999). Rethinking diversity: Hybridity and hybrid language practices in the third space. *Mind, Culture, and Activity, 6*(4), 286–303.

Holmes, B. J. (1990). New strategies are needed to produce minority teachers. In A. Dorman (Ed.), *Recruiting and retaining minority teachers* (Guest commentary). Policy Brief No. 8. North Central Regional Educational Laboratory.

hooks, b. (1994). *Teaching to transgress: Education as the practice of freedom.* Routledge.

Howard, T. C. (2001). Telling their side of the story: African American students' perceptions of culturally relevant pedagogy. *Urban Review, 33*(2), 131–149.

Howard, T. C. (2010). *Why race and culture matter in schools: Closing the achievement gap in America's classrooms.* Teachers College Press.

Howard, T. C., & Milner, H. R. (2021). Teacher preparation for urban schools. In H. R. Milner & K. Lomotey (Eds.), *Handbook of urban education* (pp. 195–211). Routledge.

Huguley, J. P., Wang, M. T., Vasquez, A. C., & Guo, J. (2019). Parental ethnic–racial socialization practices and the construction of children of color's ethnic–racial identity: A research synthesis and meta-analysis. *Psychological Bulletin, 145*(5), 437–458.

Irizarry, J. G., & Donaldson, M. L. (2012). Teach for América: The Latinization of U.S. schools and the critical shortage of Latina/o teachers. *American Educational Research Journal, 49*(1), 155–194.

Irvine, J. J. (1990). *Black students and school failure. Policies, practices, and prescriptions.* Greenwood Press.

Irvine, J. J. (2003). *Educating teachers for diversity: Seeing with a cultural eye.* Teachers College Press.

Irvine, J. J., & Irvine, R. W. (2007). The impact of the desegregation process on the education of Black students: A retrospective analysis. *Journal of Negro Education, 76*(3), 297–305.

Irvine, R. W., & Irvine, J. J. (1983). The impact of the desegregation process on the education of Black students: Key variables. *Journal of Negro Education, 52*, 410–422.

King, J. E. (1991). Dysconscious racism: Ideology, identity, and the miseducation of teachers. *Journal of Negro Education, 60*(2), 133–146.

King, S. (1993). The limited presence of African-American teachers. *Review of Educational Research, 63*(2), 115–149.

King K. V., Zucker S. (2005). *Curriculum narrowing.* Harcourt Assessment.

Ladson-Billings, G. (1992). Liberatory consequences of literacy: A case of culturally relevant instruction for African American students. *Journal of Negro Education, 61*(3), 378–391.

Ladson-Billings, G. (1994). *The dreamkeepers: Successful teachers of African-American children.* Jossey-Bass.

Ladson-Billings, G. (2006). "Yes, but how do we do it?" Practicing culturally relevant pedagogy. In J. G. Landsman & C. W. Lewis (Eds.), *White teachers diverse classrooms: Creating inclusive schools, building on students' diversity, and providing true educational equity* (pp. 33–46). Stylus.

Ladson-Billings, G. (2009). *The dreamkeepers: Successful teachers of African-American children* (2nd ed.). Jossey-Bass.

Lee, C. D. (2007). *Culture, literacy, and learning: Taking bloom in the midst of the whirlwind.* Teachers College Press.

Losen, D. J. (2011). *Discipline policies, successful schools, and racial justice.* National Education Policy Center. http://nepc.colorado.edu/publication/discipline-policies

Mathis, W. (2012). *Research-based options for education policymaking.* National Education Policy Center. http://nepc.colorado.edu/files/pb-options-2-commcore-final.pdf

McCutcheon, G. (2002). *Developing the curriculum: Solo and group deliberation.* Educators' Press International.

Meier, K. J., Stewart, J., & England, R. E. (1989). *Race, class, and education: The politics of second-generation discrimination.* University of Wisconsin Press.

Milner, H. R. (2003). Teacher reflection and race in cultural contexts: History, meaning, and methods in teaching. *Theory Into Practice, 42*(3), 173–180.

Milner, H. R. (2012). Beyond a test score: Explaining opportunity gaps in educational practice. *Journal of Black Studies, 43*(6), 693–718.

Milner, H. R. (2013). *Policy reforms and deprofessionalization of teaching.* National Education Policy Center.

Milner, H. R. (2016). A Black male teacher's culturally responsive practices. *Journal of Negro Education, 85*(4), 417–432.

Milner, H. R. (2020). *Start where you are but don't stay there: Understanding diversity, opportunity gaps, and teaching in today's classrooms* (2nd ed.). Harvard Education Press.

Milner, H. R., Cunningham, H. B., Delale-O'Connor, L., & Kestenberg, E. G. (2018). *"These kids are out of control": Why we must reimagine "classroom management" for equity.* Corwin.

Milner, H. R., & Howard, T. C. (2004). Black teachers, Black students, Black communities and *Brown*: Perspectives and insights from experts. *Journal of Negro Education, 73*(3), 285–297.

Noguera, P. A. (2003). Schools, prisons, and social implications of punishment: Rethinking disciplinary practices. *Theory Into Practice, 42*(4), 341–350.

Shujaa, M. J. (1998). *Too much schooling, too little education: A paradox of black life in white societies.* African World Press.

Shulman, L. S. (1987). Knowledge and teaching: Foundations of the new reform. *Harvard Educational Review, 19*(12), 4–14.

Skiba, R. J., Michael, R. S., Nardo, A. C., & Peterson, R. L. (2002). The color of discipline: Sources of racial and gender disproportionality in school punishment. *Urban Review, 34*(4), 317–342.

Skiba, R. J., Peterson, R. L., & Williams, T. (1997). Office referrals and suspension: Disciplinary

intervention in middle schools. *Education and Treatment of Children, 20,* 295–315.

Sleeter, C. E. (2008). Preparing white teachers for diverse students. In M. S. Khine & Y. Liu (Eds.), *Handbook of research on teacher education* (pp. 559–582). Routledge.

Sleeter, C. E., & Milner, H. R. (2011). Researching successful efforts in teacher education to diversify teachers. In A. F. Ball & C. A. Tyson (Eds.), *Studying diversity in teacher education* (81–103). American Educational Research Association.

Smagorinsky, P., Lakly, A., & Johnson, T. S. (2002). Acquiescence, accommodation, and resistance in learning to teach within a prescribed curriculum. *English Education, 34*(3), 187–211.

Tillman, L. C. (2004). (Un)Intended consequences? The impact of *Brown v. Board of Education* decision on the employment status of Black educators. *Education and Urban Society, 36*(3), 280–303.

U.S. Department of Education, Office for Civil Rights. (2014, March). *Civil rights data collection. Data snapshot: Early childhood education* (Issue Brief No. 2). https://www2.ed.gov/about/offices/list/ocr/docs/crdc-early-learning-snapshot.pdf

U.S. Department of Education, Office for Civil Rights. (2018). *Civil rights data collection. 2013-2014 state and national estimations.* https://ocrdata.ed.gov/State NationalEstimations/Estimations _2013_14

Walker, V. S. (1996). *Their highest potential: An African American school community in the segregated South.* University of North Carolina Press.

Walker, V. S. (2000). Valued segregated schools for African American children in the South, 1935–1969: A review of common themes and characteristics. *Review of Educational Research, 70*(3), 253–285.

Walker, V. S. (2013). Ninth annual Brown lecture in education research: Black educators as educational advocates in the decades before *Brown v. Board of Education. Educational Researcher, 42*(4), 207–222.

Welsh, R. O., & Little, S. (2018). The school discipline dilemma: A comprehensive review of disparities and alternative approaches. *Review of Educational Research, 88*(5), 752–794.

West, C. (1993). *Race matters.* Beacon Press.

Winn, M. T. (2018). *Justice on both sides: Transforming education through restorative justice.* Harvard Education Press.

Woolfolk, A. (2019). *Educational psychology* (14th ed.). Pearson.

Zeichner, K. M. (2003). The adequacies and inadequacies of three current strategies to recruit, prepare, and retain the best teachers for all students. *Teachers College Record, 105*(3), 490–519.

Chapter 5

Gordon, B. M. (1990). The necessity of African-American epistemology for educational theory and practice. *Journal of Education, 172*(3), 88–106.

Johnson, L. (2002). "My eyes have been opened": White teachers and racial awareness. *Journal of Teacher Education, 53*(2), 153–167.

Index

A SAGE Publishing Company

Helping educators make the greatest impact

CORWIN HAS ONE MISSION: to enhance education through intentional professional learning.

We build long-term relationships with our authors, educators, clients, and associations who partner with us to develop and continuously improve the best evidence-based practices that establish and support lifelong learning.

Solutions YOU WANT | Experts YOU TRUST | Results YOU NEED

INSTITUTES

Corwin Institutes provide regional and virtual events where educators collaborate with peers and learn from industry experts. Prepare to be recharged and motivated!

corwin.com/institutes

ON-SITE PROFESSIONAL LEARNING

Corwin on-site PD is delivered through high-energy keynotes, practical workshops, and custom coaching services designed to support knowledge development and implementation.

www.corwin.com/pd

VIRTUAL PROFESSIONAL LEARNING

Our virtual PD combines live expert facilitation with the flexibility of anytime, anywhere professional learning. See the power of intentionally designed virtual PD.

www.corwin.com/virtualworkshops

CORWIN ONLINE

Online learning designed to engage, inform, challenge, and inspire. Our courses offer practical, classroom-focused instruction that will meet your continuing education needs and enhance your practice.

www.corwinonline.com

Visit www.corwin.com

CORWIN